SIDE by SIDE

THIRD EDITION

BOOK 2

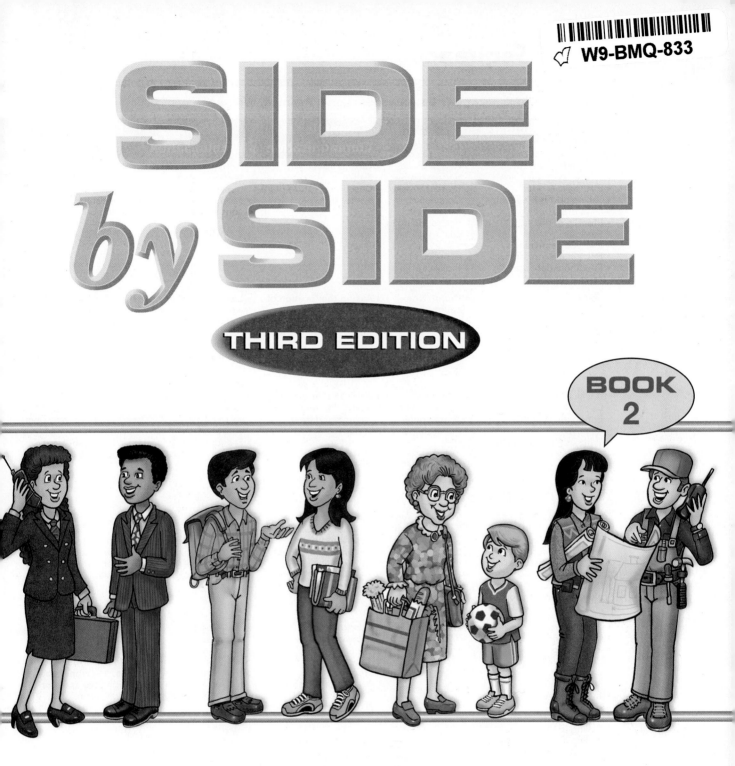

Steven J. Molinsky
Bill Bliss

Illustrated by

Richard E. Hill

Scope and Sequence

Chapter	Topics, Vocabulary, & Math	Grammar	Functional Communication	Listening & Pronunciation	Writing
1	• Describing present, past, & future actions • Birthdays & gifts • Telling about friendships • Days of the week • Months of the year • Seasons • Everyday activities • Past time expressions • Reading a date using ordinal numbers	• Review of tenses: Simple Present, Present Continuous, Simple Past, Future: Going to • Like to • Time expressions • Indirect object pronouns	• Talking about likes & dislikes • Describing future plans & intentions	• Listening for correct tense in information questions • Pronouncing contrastive stress	• Writing about your last birthday • Writing about a friendship • Filling out a personal information form
2	• Food • Buying food • Being a guest at mealtime • Describing food preferences	• Count/Non-count nouns	• Asking the location of items • Making a suggestion • Complimenting about food	• Listening for key words to determine subject matter of conversations • Pronouncing reduced *for*	• Making a list of foods in the kitchen and their location • Writing about favorite foods • Writing about school
3	• Buying food • Describing food • Eating in a restaurant • Recipes • Units of measure & their abbreviations • Dollar amounts expressed in numerals	• Partitives • Count/Non-count nouns • Imperatives	• Asking for information • Asking for and making recommendations about food • Giving and following instructions	• Listening for key words to determine subject matter of conversations • Pronouncing *of* before consonants & vowels	• Making a shopping list • Writing a recipe • Writing about a special meal • Writing about a supermarket
Gazette	• Food shopping • Ordering fast food • Interpreting statistics about food consumption • Culture concept: Where people shop for food around the world	• Simple past tense • Present tense • Count/Non-count nouns	• Describing people's customs & consumer behavior	• Listening to & interpreting announcements in a supermarket correctly	• Writing an e-mail or instant message to tell about the meals you eat
4	• Telling about the future • Identifying life events • Identifying health problems & injuries • Probability • Possibility • Talking about favorite seasons • Warnings • Calling in sick • Calling a school to report a child's absence	• Future tense: Will • Time expressions • Might	• Asking about & giving information about future events • Asking for and making predictions • Asking for repetition • Expressing fears • Providing reassurance	• Listening to & responding appropriately to a speaker in a telephone conversation • Pronouncing *going to*	• Writing a note to a child's teacher to explain an absence • Writing about your future—where you might live and work, and what might happen in your life • Writing about plans for the weekend
5	• Making comparisons • Advice • Expressing opinions • Agreement & disagreement • Teenager & parent relationships • Community features & problems	• Comparatives • Should • Possessive pronouns	• Asking for & giving advice • Agreeing & disagreeing • Comparing things, places, & people • Exchanging opinions	• Listening to determine the subject matter of a conversation • Pronouncing yes/no questions with *or*	• Writing about a comparison of two places

LIFESKILLS, TEST PREPARATION, CURRICULUM STANDARDS & FRAMEWORKS

Lifeskills & Test Preparation	EFF	SCANS/Employment Competencies	CASAS	LAUSD	LCPs
• Asking & answering personal information questions • Providing information about family members • Calendars, dates, & ordinal numbers • Writing months, days, & dates • Writing ordinal numbers	• Interact in a way that is friendly • Identify family relationships • Identify supportive friendships	• Sociability • Allocate time	0.1.2, 0.1.6, 0.2.1, 0.2.2, 0.2.4	1, 2, 3, 4, 5, 6, 7a, 11e	39.01, 39.02, 39.04, 49.03, 50.02
• School personnel & locations • Classroom instructions • Computer components • School registration • Reading a class schedule • The education system • Learning skills: Chronological order, Steps in a process	• Manage resources: Identify those resources you have; Determine where they are	• Identify resources • Understand an organizational system (a school; the education system) • Work with technology	0.1.2, 0.1.4, 0.1.5, 2.5.5, 4.5.1, 4.5.2	9a, 10c, 12, 13, 14, 15, 59, 60, 61	38.01, 39.04, 41.06, 48.02, 48.03, 50.07
• Food containers & quantities • Food weights & measures: Abbreviations • Asking about availability & location of items in a store • Food advertisements • Food packaging & label information • Reading a supermarket receipt • Reading a menu & computing costs • Ordering a meal	• Manage resources • Understand, interpret, & work with numbers	• Identify resources • Allocate money • Serve clients/customers	0.1.2, 0.1.3, 1.1.4, 1.1.7, 1.2.1, 1.2.2, 1.3.8, 1.3.9, 1.6.1, 2.6.4, 3.5.1, 6.6.4, 8.1.4	27, 30, 31, 32, 34, 35, 36	41.06, 42.02, 45.01, 45.03, 49.14, 50.07
• Interpreting a narrative reading about people's customs & consumer behavior • Interpreting statistical facts • Ordering fast food • Interpreting announcements over a store P.A. system	• Analyze & use information • Identify community needs & resources • Respect others & value diversity	• Acquire & evaluate information • Identify resources • Work with cultural diversity	0.1.2, 1.1.7, 1.3.8	34, 36	41.06, 49.12, 50.02, 50.07
• Small talk at work & at school • Invitations & offers • Asking for clarification	• Manage resources: Determine time of future events • Interact in a way that is friendly • Seek input from others • Identify problems • Provide for family members' needs • Create a vision & goals for the future	• Sociability • Identify goal-relevant activities • Identify workplace safety problems & state warnings • Self-management • Responsibility	0.1.2, 0.1.4, 0.1.6, 0.2.4, 2.5.5, 4.4.1	7, 9, 11, 16a, 55a	36.01, 36.02, 36.03, 36.04, 36.05, 37.04, 41.03, 49.12, 50.02
• Small talk at work & at school • Compliments • Appropriate language in social situations • Thank-you notes • Expressing opinions	• Interact in a way that is friendly • Seek input from others • Guide & support others • Identify supportive family relationships • Meet family needs & responsibilities • Advocate & influence	• Sociability • Decision making • Understand a social system (community)	0.1.2, 0.1.4, 0.2.4	7, 10	37.04, 39.02, 39.03, 39.04, 50.04

EFF: Equipped for the Future (Content standards, Common activities, & Key activities for Citizen/Community Member, Worker, & Parent/Family role maps; EFF Communication and Reflection/Evaluation skills are covered in every chapter)

SCANS: Secretary's Commission on Achieving Necessary Skills (U.S. Department of Labor)

CASAS: Comprehensive Adult Student Assessment System

LAUSD: Los Angeles Unified School District (ESL Beginning High content standards)

LCPs: Literacy Completion Points (Florida & Texas: Level C Workforce Development Skills & Life Skills. The following LCPs are covered throughout the text: 49.01–49.17, 50.01–50.08, 51.01–51.05)

Scope and Sequence

Chapter	Topics, Vocabulary, & Math	Grammar	Functional Communication	Listening & Pronunciation	Writing
6	• Describing people, places, & things • Identifying positive & negative personal qualities • Expressing pride in a child's personal qualities • Shopping in a department store • Expressing opinions • Identifying different types of stores and comparing prices, quality of products, convenience, & service	• Superlatives	• Expressing an opinion • Offering assistance	• Listening to determine a speaker's attitude or opinion • Pronouncing linking words with duplicated consonants	• Writing about the most important person in your life
Gazette	• Interpreting numerical and descriptive facts about world records and geographic features • Culture concept: Recreation & entertainment around the world	• Superlatives • Adjectives with negative prefixes	• Interpreting factual statements • Describing	• Listening to and interpreting radio advertisements correctly	• Writing an e-mail or instant message to tell about a favorite vacation place
7	• Getting around town • Places in the community • Public transportation • Following a map or diagram indicating directions to a destination	• Imperatives • Directions	• Giving & following instructions • Asking for repetition • Asking for & giving recommendations	• Listening for specific information in directions • Listening to make deductions about the location of conversations • Pronouncing *could you* & *would you*	• Drawing a map & writing directions to your home • Writing about how to get to different places in the community
8	• Describing people's actions • Occupations • Asking for & giving feedback about job performance • Identifying ways to improve performance at work & at school • Describing plans & intentions • Consequences of actions • Superstitions	• Adverbs • Comparative of adverbs • Agent nouns • If-clauses	• Expressing an opinion • Expressing agreement • Asking for & giving feedback • Asking about & giving information about future plans • Giving & receiving advice	• Listening to determine the correct consequences of actions • Pronouncing contrastive stress	• Writing about something you want to do and the consequences of doing it • Filling out a job application form
Gazette	• Tips for a successful job interview • Occupations • Culture concept: Men's & women's jobs in different countries	• Adverbs • Agent nouns	• Interpreting advice • Describing self	• Listening to & interpreting announcements at a workplace correctly	• Writing an e-mail or instant message to tell about your skills & activities
9	• Describing ongoing past activities • Giving information about a robbery • Describing a mishap • Describing an accident	• Past continuous tense • Reflexive pronouns • While-clauses	• Asking about & giving information about past events • Expressing concern about someone • Expressing sympathy • Reacting to bad news • Describing a sequence of events	• Listening to make deductions about the context of conversations • Pronouncing *did* & *was*	• Writing about preference for doing things alone or with other people

Lifeskills & Test Preparation	EFF	SCANS/Employment Competencies	CASAS	LAUSD	LCPs
• Shopping requests & locating items • Understanding ATM instructions • Interpreting a check • Problems with purchases • Returning & exchanging items • Store sales • Filling out a check • Learning skill: Steps in a process	• Interact in a way that is friendly • Identify a strong sense of family • Advocate & influence • Identify community resources • Use technology to accomplish goals	• Sociability • Integrity/Honesty • Serve clients/customers • Identify resources	0.1.3, 0.1.4, 1.3.3, 1.3.9, 1.6.3, 1.8.1, 1.8.2, 8.1.4	10a, 28, 29, 30, 33, 59	42.03, 42.05, 45.01, 45.04, 45.06, 50.04
• Interpreting statistical facts • Interpreting radio advertisements	• Analyze & use information • Understand, interpret, & work with numbers • Respect others & value diversity	• Acquire & evaluate information • Work with cultural diversity	0.1.3, 1.3.9	30	49.04, 49.12, 50.04
• Interpreting schedules in the community • Locating places on a map • Compass directions • Reading a bus schedule • Highway & traffic signs & symbols • Police commands & traffic signs • Postal services • Simple written directions • Drawing a map	• Identify community resources • Seek & receive assistance • Give direction • Understand, interpret, & work with numbers & symbolic information	• Identify resources • Communicate information • See things in the mind's eye (Interpret a simple route map; Draw a simple route map)	0.1.2, 1.1.4, 1.9.1, 2.2.1, 2.2.2, 2.4.2, 2.4.4, 2.5.4, 2.6.1, 2.6.2, 6.6.4	8a, 22, 23, 24, 31, 41, 42	36.04, 43.01, 43.02, 43.03, 46.01, 46.02, 49.09, 49.14
• Help wanted ads • Job interview questions about skills & work history • Describing a work schedule • Calling in sick & late • Requesting a schedule change • Employee accident reports • Reading a paycheck stub • Nonverbal behavior at the job interview	• Cooperate with others • Work together • Seek input from others • Guide & support others • Work within the big picture • Create goals • Reflect & evaluate	• Participate as a member of a team • Self-management: Monitor progress • Responsibility • Decision making • Self-esteem	0.1.3, 0.2.1, 0.2.2, 4.1.2, 4.1.3, 4.1.5, 4.1.6, 4.1.7, 4.2.1, 4.3.4, 4.4.1, 4.4.3, 4.6.5	8, 51, 52, 53, 54, 55, 56, 57	35.01, 35.02, 35.03, 35.04, 35.05, 35.06, 35.07, 36.01, 36.02, 36.05, 36.06, 50.05
• Identifying appropriate job interview behaviors, including dress, promptness, eye contact, speaking style, honesty, & confidence • Identifying occupations • Interpreting announcements over a workplace P.A. system	• Analyze & use information • Develop & express sense of self • Interact in a way that is friendly & courteous • Respect others & value diversity	• Acquire & evaluate information • Self-esteem • Integrity/Honesty • Sociability • Work with cultural diversity	0.2.1, 4.1.5, 4.1.6, 4.1.7	53, 54	35.01, 35.02, 35.06, 37.04, 49.12, 50.05
• First-aid kit • Calling 911 • Describing a suspect's physical characteristics to the police • Warning labels on household products • First-aid procedures • Learning skills: Categorizing words, Word sets	• Interact in a way that is friendly • Identify problems • Develop & express sense of self • Identify resources • Provide for family members' safety & physical needs	• Sociability • Self-esteem • Communicate information	0.1.2, 0.1.4, 0.2.2, 0.2.4, 2.1.2, 3.4.1, 3.4.3, 7.2.3	3, 6, 7a, 7b, 10b, 20, 49, 50, 64	39.02, 40.03, 44.01, 49.03, 49.08, 50.02

Scope and Sequence

Chapter	Topics, Vocabulary, & Math	Grammar	Functional Communication	Listening & Pronunciation	Writing
10	• Describing physical states & emotions • Expressing past & future ability • Expressing past & future obligation • Giving an excuse • Household problems	• Could • Be able to • Have got to • Too + adjective	• Asking and telling about ability to do things • Expressing obligation	• Listening for correct situation or context • Pronouncing *have to* & *have got to*	• Writing about a time you were frustrated, disappointed, or upset • Writing about an apartment or home
Gazette	• Families & time • Interpreting a table with number facts • Home appliances • Culture concept: Child-care around the world	• Tense review • Have to / Have got to	• Describing daily life & customs	• Listening to messages on a telephone answering machine	• Writing an e-mail or instant message to tell about activities and occurrences during the week
11	• Medical examinations • Medical advice • Health • Foods • Nutrition • Home remedies	• Past tense review • Count/Non-count noun review • Must • Mustn't vs. Don't have to • Must vs. Should	• Asking for & giving advice • Describing a future sequence of events • Describing a past sequence of events • Expressing concern	• Listening for key words to determine subject matter of conversations • Pronouncing *must* & *mustn't*	• Making a list of healthy and unhealthy foods • Writing about rules in life—at school, on the job, at home, in the community • Filling out a medical history form
12	• Everyday activities • Describing future activities • Expressing time & duration • Making plans by telephone • Borrowing & returning items • Life cycle—stages & events • Holidays • Family members	• Future continuous tense • Time expressions	• Asking and telling about future plans & activities • Calling people on the telephone	• Listening to messages on a telephone answering machine • Pronouncing contractions with *will*	• Writing about a family holiday celebration
13	• Offering help • Indicating ownership • Neighbors • Household problems • Using the telephone to secure household repair services • Car trouble • Friends	• Some/Any • Pronoun review • Verb tense review	• Offering help • Asking & telling about past events • Asking for & giving advice • Describing problems	• Listening for correct pronouns in conversations • Listening to make deductions about the subject of conversations • Pronouncing deleted *h*	• Writing about relying on friends for help • Writing about a very good friend
Gazette	• Communities—urban, suburban, & rural • Interpreting a bar graph with population data in millions • Household repair people • Culture concept: Where friends gather in different countries around the world	• Present tense review • Future tense review	• Describing community life • Describing future events	• Listening to telephone conversations & answering machine messages to make deductions about the subject of conversations	• Writing an e-mail or instant message to tell about a future family celebration

Lifeskills & Test Preparation	EFF	SCANS/Employment Competencies	CASAS	LAUSD	LCPs
• Housing ads • Inquiring about rentals • Describing maintenance & repairs needed in a rental unit • Reading a floor plan/diagram	• Interact in a way that is tactful • Identify supportive friendships • Reflect & evaluate	• Sociability • Self-esteem • See things in the mind's eye (Interpret a diagram)	0.1.2, 0.1.4, 1.4.2, 1.4.7, 7.4.1	7b, 9b, 10a, 37, 38, 39, 62	39.03, 45.07, 45.08, 49.09, 50.04
• Interpreting a narrative reading about daily life & customs • Interpreting statistical facts in a table • Interpreting telephone messages on an answering machine	• Analyze & use information • Identify supportive family relationships • Meet family needs & responsibilities • Understand, interpret, & work with numbers • Respect others & value diversity • Use technology & other tools to accomplish goals	• Acquire & evaluate information • Work with cultural diversity • Work with technology (telephone answering device)	0.1.2, 0.2.4, 2.1.7, 7.4.1	7a, 18, 62	40.02, 48.04, 49.09, 49.12, 50.02
• Identifying parts of the face & body • Common symptoms • Calling to report an absence • Making a doctor appointment • Procedures during a medical exam • Common prescription & non-prescription medicines • Interpreting medicine label dosages & instructions • A note to the teacher explaining a child's absence	• Seek guidance & support from others • Guide & support others • Meet family needs & responsibilities	• Acquire & evaluate information • Self-management • Understand a social system	0.1.2, 2.5.5, 3.1.1, 3.1.2, 3.2.1, 3.3.1, 3.3.2, 3.3.3	16, 43, 44, 45, 46, 47	41.01, 41.03, 41.04, 41.06, 48.01, 50.02, 50.07
• Fahrenheit & celsius temperatures • Temperature values • Beginning & ending a telephone conversation • Using the telephone directory: White pages, Government pages, & Yellow pages • Phone messages • Recorded telephone information	• Interact in a way that is friendly & courteous • Manage resources: Allocate time • Create a vision for the future • Identify family relationships • Identify a strong sense of family • Gather information • Identify community resources	• Identify goal-relevant activities • Allocate time • Self-esteem • Acquire & evaluate information • Identify resources • Work with technology (recorded telephone announcements)	0.1.4, 0.2.4, 1.1.5, 2.1.1, 2.1.7, 2.1.8, 2.3.2, 7.4.5	7a, 9, 17, 18, 19, 21, 25, 26, 58	39.02, 40.02, 40.04, 46.04, 47.01, 47.02, 50.02
• Household repair problems • Securing household repair services • Reading a TV schedule • Recorded telephone instructions • Making a schedule	• Identify problems • Interact in a way that is tactful • Identify supportive friendships • Identify problems • Seek & receive assistance	• Participate as a member of a team • Understand a social system (an apartment building & neighbors) • Identify resources • Work with technology (recorded telephone instructions)	1.4.7, 2.1.7, 2.1.8, 2.6.1, 2.6.2	17, 18, 22, 39, 63	39.02, 39.03, 40.02, 40.04, 42.01, 45.08, 49.09, 50.02
• Interpreting a narrative reading about types of communities • Interpreting statistical facts in a bar graph • Identifying home repair needs & home repair services	• Analyze & use information • Identify community needs & resources • Understand, interpret, & work with numbers & symbolic information • Respect others & value diversity • Use technology & other tools to accomplish goals	• Acquire & evaluate information • Understand a social system (communities) • See things in the mind's eye (Interpret a bar graph) • Work with cultural diversity	0.1.2, 0.2.4, 1.4.7, 7.4.1	7a, 39, 62	49.03, 49.09, 49.12, 50.02

Dear Friends,

Thank you for choosing Side by Side as your English textbook!

The mission of Side by Side has always been to offer learners a dynamic and communicative approach to help them develop the language skills they need in order to use English effectively in daily life, in the community, in school, at work, and in general, to achieve their hopes and dreams.

While the curriculum comprehensively integrates lifeskills, workplace communication, and other relevant topics, Side by Side is solidly and proudly a grammar-based program that attempts to build upon our profession's most important developments in research and practice over the decades. The text's research-based grammatical sequence is rooted in the important work of linguists of the 1940s and 1950s. Its instructional methodology reflects the exciting innovations in communicative language teaching that emerged in the 1960s and 1970s. And the 21st-century relevance of its lifeskill topics is based on the past three decades of development of competency-based approaches to language instruction, including current national, state, and local standards-based curricula you can find in the Scope & Sequence on the previous pages.

The core methodology of Side by Side's communicative approach is the guided conversation – the brief dialog that engages students in meaningful conversational exchanges within carefully structured frameworks, and then encourages students to break away from the text and use these frameworks to create conversations on their own. This practice becomes the context and springboard for the reading, writing, listening, pronunciation, role-playing, and discussion activities that follow.

Our objective is to help you create a classroom environment in which students dynamically interact with each other – working together to develop their language skills "side by side." We also believe that language instruction is most powerful when it is joyful. There is magic in the power of humor, fun, games, and music to encourage students to take risks with their emerging language, to "play" with it, and to allow their personalities to shine through as their language skills increase.

As a new generation of language learners now uses this program, we believe more strongly than ever that as we meet the demands to fill our lesson plans with competencies and content, we must also take care to preserve our role as true teachers of language – helping students develop the competence and confidence to use English creatively to meet their own needs, life circumstances, and goals – today and in the future.

We are deeply honored by your support over the years, and we promise to continue working hard to help you provide students with a language learning experience that is dynamic . . . interactive . . . and fun!

Steven J. Molinsky
Bill Bliss

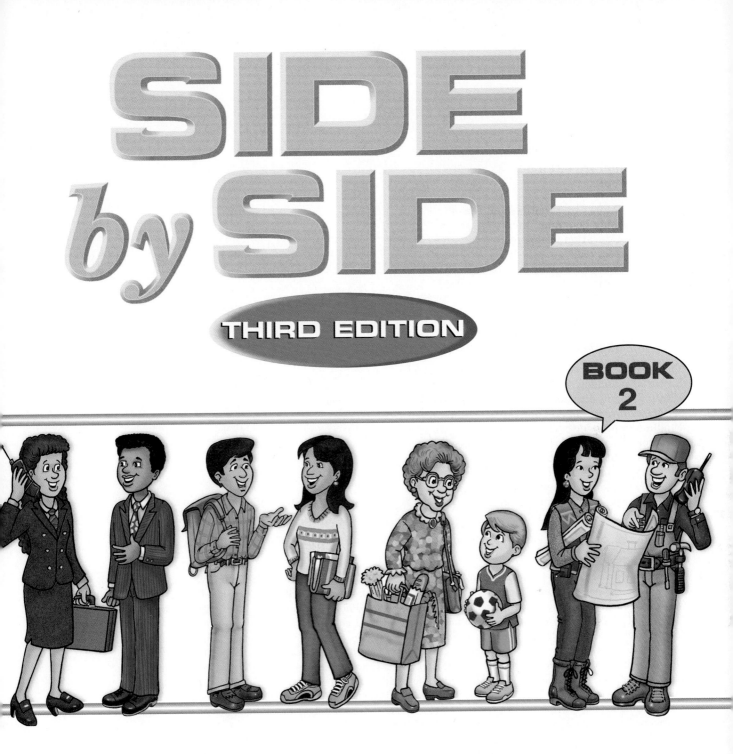

SIDE by SIDE

THIRD EDITION

BOOK 2

Steven J. Molinsky
Bill Bliss

Illustrated by

Richard E. Hill

Side by Side, 3rd edition
Student Book 2

Pearson Education, 10 Bank Street, White Plains, NY 10606

Vice president, director of publishing: *Allen Ascher*
Editorial manager: *Pam Fishman*
Vice president, director of design and production: *Rhea Banker*
Associate director of electronic production: *Aliza Greenblatt*
Production manager: *Ray Keating*
Director of manufacturing: *Patrice Fraccio*
Digital layout specialist: *Wendy Wolf*
Associate art director: *Elizabeth Carlson*
Interior design: *Elizabeth Carlson, Wendy Wolf*
Cover design: *Elizabeth Carlson*
Copyediting: *Janet Johnston*

Contributing *Side by Side* Gazette authors: *Laura English, Meredith Westfall*

Photo credits: p. 27, (*left*) David Young-Wolff/PhotoEdit, (*right*) Rudy Von Briel/PhotoEdit; p. 28 (*top*) Cosmo Condina/Stone, (*bottom*) David Young Wolff/PhotoEdit, (*center*) Don Smetzer/Stone; p. 59, (*top*) Courtesy Guinness World Records, Ltd., (*center, left*) Inacio Teixeira/AP/Wide World Photos, (*center, right*) Hugh Sitton/Stone, (*bottom, left*) Chad Ehlers/Stone; p. 60, (*top*) Ray Stott/The Image Works, (*center*) Margot Granitsas/The Image Works, (*bottom*) Popperfoto/Archive Photos; p. 81, SuperStock, Inc.; p. 82, (*top, left*) ©Steve Raymer/CORBIS, (*top, right*) ©Martin Rogers/CORBIS, (*center, left*) S. Noorani/Woodfin Camp & Associates, (*right, center*) Vo-Trung Dung/Woodfin Camp & Associates, (*bottom, left*) Capital Features/The Image Works, (*bottom, right*) Ranald Mackechnie/Stone; p. 103, (*center*) Tom McCarthy/PhotoEdit, (*right*) Owen Franken/Stock Boston, (*left*) Jose Pelaez/The Stock Market; p. 104, (*top*) Seth Resnick/Stock Boston, (*center*) Bob Daemmrich/The Image Works, (*bottom*) Stephanie Maze/Corbis; p. 137 photo credit to come, p. 138, (*top*) Robert Fried/Stock Boston, (*bottom*) Fritz Hoffmann/The Image Works, (*center*) Bill Bachmann/PhotoEdit.

The authors gratefully acknowledge the contribution of Tina Carver in the development of the original *Side by Side* program.

ISBN 0-13-026757-0   (Regular Edition)

18 19 – V082 – 13 12 11 10

ISBN 0-13-111960-5   (Regular Edition with Audio Highlights)

8 9 10 11 12 13 14 – V082 – 13 12 11 10 09 08

ISBN 0-13-183935-7   (International Edition)

11 12 13 14 15 16 17 – V082 – 13 12 11 10 09 08

How to Say It! (Communication Strategies)

Pronunciation

1

Review of Tenses:
Simple Present
Present Continuous
Simple Past
Future: Going to

Like to
Time Expressions
Indirect Object
Pronouns

- **Describing Present, Past, and Future Actions**

- **Birthdays and Gifts**
- **Telling About Friendships**

VOCABULARY PREVIEW

Spring

Summer

Fall

Winter

1. **Days of the Week**
   Sunday
   Monday
   Tuesday
   Wednesday
   Thursday
   Friday
   Saturday

2. **Months of the Year**
   January   July
   February   August
   March   September
   April   October
   May   November
   June   December

3. **Seasons**
   spring
   summer
   fall / autumn
   winter

What Do You Like to Do on the Weekend?

I We You They	like to	
		eat.
He She It	likes to	

A. What do you like to do on the weekend?

B. I like to read.

A. What does Ron like to do on the weekend?

B. He likes to go to the mall.

1. *Mr. and Mrs. Johnson?*
   watch TV

2. *Tom?*
   play basketball

3. *Sally?*
   go to the beach

4. *you and your friends?*
   chat online

5. *your grandmother?*
   go hiking

6. *you?*

TALK ABOUT IT! *What Do They Like to Do?*

cook	play	swim	write
cooks	plays	swims	writes
cooked	played	swam	wrote
cooking	playing	swimming	writing

Robert likes to cook.
He cooks every day.
He cooked yesterday.
He's cooking right now.
He's going to cook tomorrow.
As you can see, Robert REALLY likes to cook.

Irene likes to play the piano.
She plays the piano every day.
She played the piano yesterday.
She's playing the piano right now.
She's going to play the piano tomorrow.
As you can see, Irene REALLY likes to play
    the piano.

Jimmy and Patty like to swim.*
They swim every day.
They swam yesterday.
They're swimming right now.
They're going to swim tomorrow.
As you can see, Jimmy and Patty REALLY
    like to swim.

Jonathan likes to write.
He writes every day.
He wrote yesterday.
He's writing right now.
He's going to write tomorrow.
As you can see, Jonathan REALLY likes to
    write.

Using these questions, talk about the people above with students in your class.

What does _____ like to do?
What does he/she do every day?
What did he/she do yesterday?
What's he/she doing right now?
What's he/she going to do tomorrow?

What do _____ like to do?
What do they do every day?
What did they do yesterday?
What are they doing right now?
What are they going to do tomorrow?

Then use these questions to talk about other people you know.

* swim – swam

3

Are You Going to Cook Spaghetti This Week?

A. Are you going to cook spaghetti this week?

B. No, I'm not. I cooked spaghetti LAST week, and I don't like to cook spaghetti very often.

1. Are you going to watch videos today?

2. Are you going to drive downtown this weekend?

3. Is Mrs. Miller going to plant flowers this spring?

4. Is your father going to make pancakes this morning?

5. Are Mr. and Mrs. Jenkins going to the mall* this Saturday?

6. Are you and your friends going skiing this December?

7. Are you going to write letters tonight?

8. Is Dave going to clean his room this week?

9. Are you and your family going to WonderWorld this year?

10.

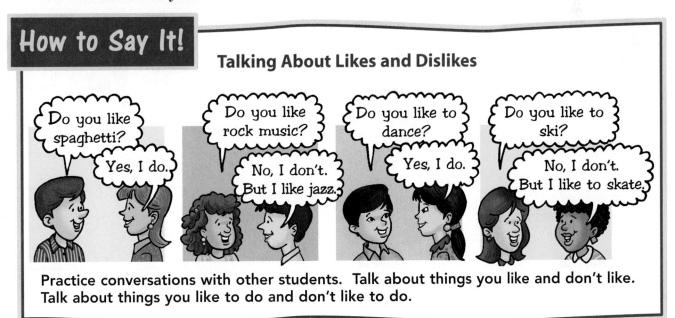

How to Say It!

Talking About Likes and Dislikes

Do you like spaghetti?

Yes, I do.

Do you like rock music?

No, I don't. But I like jazz.

Do you like to dance?

Yes, I do.

Do you like to ski?

No, I don't. But I like to skate.

Practice conversations with other students. Talk about things you like and don't like. Talk about things you like to do and don't like to do.

* going to the mall = going to go to the mall

What Are You Going to Give Your Wife?

I'm going to give { my husband / my wife } a present.　　I'm going to give { him / her } a present.

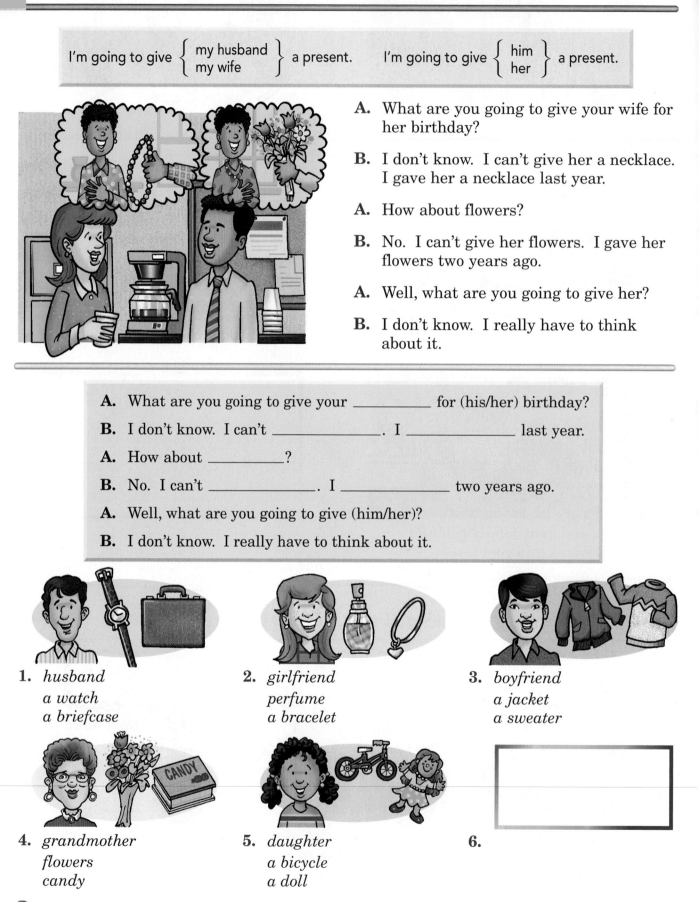

A. What are you going to give your wife for her birthday?

B. I don't know. I can't give her a necklace. I gave her a necklace last year.

A. How about flowers?

B. No. I can't give her flowers. I gave her flowers two years ago.

A. Well, what are you going to give her?

B. I don't know. I really have to think about it.

A. What are you going to give your _____ for (his/her) birthday?

B. I don't know. I can't _____. I _____ last year.

A. How about _____?

B. No. I can't _____. I _____ two years ago.

A. Well, what are you going to give (him/her)?

B. I don't know. I really have to think about it.

1. *husband*
   a watch
   a briefcase

2. *girlfriend*
   perfume
   a bracelet

3. *boyfriend*
   a jacket
   a sweater

4. *grandmother*
   flowers
   candy

5. *daughter*
   a bicycle
   a doll

6.

6

What Did Your Parents Give You?

I	me
he	him
she	her
we	us
you	you
they	them

A. What did your parents give you for your birthday?

B. They gave me a CD player.

1. What did you give your parents for their anniversary?

a painting

2. What did Mr. Lee's grandchildren give him for his birthday?

a computer

3. What did your children give you and your wife for your anniversary?

a plant

4. I forget. What did you give me for my last birthday?

a purple blouse with pink polka dots

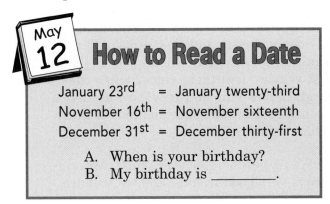

How to Read a Date

May 12

January 23rd = January twenty-third
November 16th = November sixteenth
December 31st = December thirty-first

A. When is your birthday?
B. My birthday is _____.

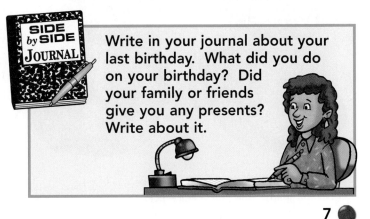

SIDE by SIDE JOURNAL

Write in your journal about your last birthday. What did you do on your birthday? Did your family or friends give you any presents? Write about it.

VERY GOOD FRIENDS: EAST AND WEST

Eric and Susan are very good friends. They grew up together, they went to high school together, and they went to college together. Now Eric lives in California, and Susan lives in New Jersey. Even though they live far apart, they're still very good friends.

They write to each other very often. He writes her letters about life on the West Coast, and she writes him letters about life on the East Coast. They never forget each other's birthday. Last year he sent* her some CDs, and she sent him a wallet. Eric and Susan help each other very often. Last year he lent* her money when she was in the hospital, and she gave him advice when he lost* his job.

Eric and Susan like each other very much. They were always very good friends, and they still are.

VERY GOOD FRIENDS: NORTH AND SOUTH

Carlos and Maria are our very good friends. For many years we went to church together, we took vacations together, and our children played together. Now Carlos and Maria live in Florida, and we still live here in Wisconsin. Even though we live far apart, we're still very good friends.

We communicate with each other very often on the Internet. We send them messages about life up north, and they send us messages about life down south. We never forget each others' anniversaries. Last year we sent them Wisconsin cheese, and they sent us Florida oranges. We also help each other very often. Last year we lent them money when they bought a new van, and they gave us advice when we sold* our house and moved into a condominium.

We like each other very much. We were always very good friends, and we still are.

* send – sent   lose – lost
  lend – lent   sell – sold

✔ READING *CHECK-UP*

True or False?

1. Eric and Susan are in high school.
2. Eric lives on the West Coast.
3. Susan sent Eric some CDs last year.
4. Susan was sick last year.
5. They were friends when they were children.
6. Carlos and Maria don't live in Wisconsin now.
7. Florida is in the north.
8. Carlos and Maria send messages on the Internet.
9. Carlos and Maria moved into a condominium last year.

LISTENING

Listen and choose the correct answer.

1. a. I like to play tennis.
   b. I'm going to play tennis.
2. a. I went to the beach.
   b. I go to the beach.
3. a. Yesterday morning.
   b. Tomorrow afternoon.
4. a. I gave them a plant.
   b. I'm going to give them a plant.
5. a. We went to the mall.
   b. We're going to the mall.
6. a. They sent messages last week.
   b. They send messages every week.
7. a. He gave her flowers.
   b. She gave him flowers.
8. a. Last weekend.
   b. Tomorrow morning.

IN YOUR OWN WORDS

For Writing and Discussion

A VERY GOOD FRIEND

Do you have a very good friend who lives far away? Tell about your friendship.

How do you know each other?
How do you communicate with each other?
  (Do you call? write? send e-mail messages?)
What do you talk about or write about?
Do you send each other presents?
Do you help each other? How?

PRONUNCIATION *Contrastive Stress*

Listen. Then say it.

I'm not going to clean my room this week.
I cleaned my room LÁST week.

I'm not going to make pancakes this morning.
I made pancakes YÉSTERDAY morning.

Say it. Then listen.

I'm not going to watch videos tonight.
I watched videos LÁST night.

I'm not going to write letters this evening.
I wrote letters YÉSTERDAY evening.

9

GRAMMAR

SIMPLE PRESENT TENSE

I We You They	cook.
He She It	cooks.

LIKE TO

I We You They	like to / don't like to	
He She It	likes to / doesn't like to	cook.

PRESENT CONTINUOUS TENSE

(I am)	I'm	
(He is) (She is) (It is)	He's She's It's	cooking.
(We are) (You are) (They are)	We're You're They're	

SIMPLE PAST TENSE

I He She It We You They	cooked.

FUTURE: GOING TO

I'm He's She's It's We're You're They're	going to cook.

Am	I	
Is	he she it	going to cook?
Are	we you they	

	I	am.
Yes,	he she it	is.
	we you they	are.

	I'm	not.
No,	he she it	isn't.
	we you they	aren't.

INDIRECT OBJECT PRONOUNS

He gave	me him her it us you them	a present.

PAST TIME EXPRESSIONS

yesterday
yesterday morning / afternoon / evening
last night
last week / weekend / month / year
last Sunday / Monday / . . . / Saturday
last January / February / . . . / December
last spring / summer / fall (autumn) / winter

IRREGULAR VERBS

drive – drove
give – gave
go – went
lend – lent
lose – lost
sell – sold
send – sent
swim – swam
write – wrote

KEY VOCABULARY

EVERYDAY ACTIVITIES

chat online
clean
cook
drive
go *hiking*
go to *the mall*
make *pancakes*
plant
play *basketball*
play the *piano*
read
swim
watch TV
write

DAYS OF THE WEEK

Sunday
Monday
Tuesday
Wednesday
Thursday
Friday
Saturday

MONTHS OF THE YEAR

January
February
March
April
May
June
July
August
September
October
November
December

SEASONS

spring
summer
fall / autumn
winter

10

Count/Non-Count Nouns

- **Food**
- **Buying Food**
- **Being a Guest at Mealtime**
- **Describing Food Preferences**

VOCABULARY PREVIEW

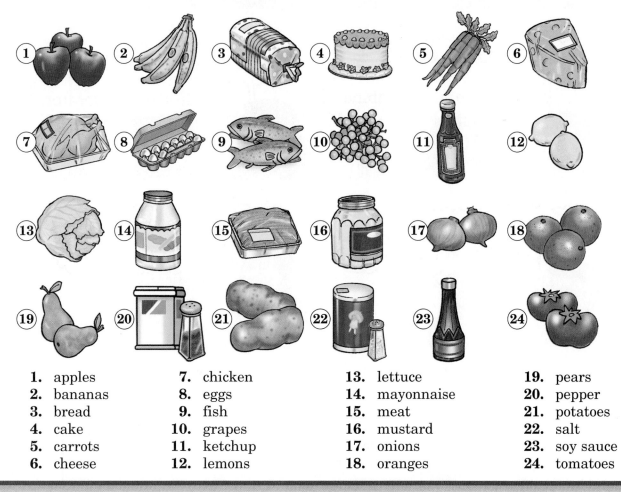

1. apples	7. chicken	13. lettuce	19. pears
2. bananas	8. eggs	14. mayonnaise	20. pepper
3. bread	9. fish	15. meat	21. potatoes
4. cake	10. grapes	16. mustard	22. salt
5. carrots	11. ketchup	17. onions	23. soy sauce
6. cheese	12. lemons	18. oranges	24. tomatoes

Practice conversations with other students. Talk about the foods in this kitchen.

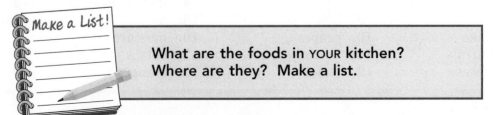

Make a List!

What are the foods in YOUR kitchen?
Where are they? Make a list.

Let's Make Sandwiches for Lunch!

Let's make sandwiches for lunch!

Sorry, we can't. There **isn't** any **bread**.

Let's make an apple pie for dessert!

Sorry, we can't. There **aren't** any **apples**.

1. Let's make pizza for lunch!
cheese

2. Let's make some fresh lemonade!
lemons

3. Let's make a salad for dinner!
lettuce

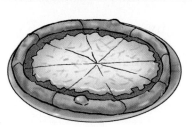

4. Let's make an omelet for breakfast!
eggs

5. Let's bake a cake for dessert!
flour

6. Let's make some fresh orange juice for breakfast!
oranges

7. Let's have french fries with our hamburgers!
potatoes

8. Let's have meatballs with our spaghetti!
meat

9.

How Much Milk Do You Want?

how much? too much	how many? too many
a little	a few

A. How much milk do you want?

B. Not too much. Just a little.

A. Okay. Here you are.

B. Thanks.

A. How many cookies do you want?

B. Not too many. Just a few.

A. Okay. Here you are.

B. Thanks.

1. *rice*

2. *french fries*

3. *ice cream*

4. *coffee*

5. *meatballs*

6.

ROLE PLAY *Would You Care for Some More?*

Some of your friends are having dinner at your home. How do they like the food? Ask them.

A. How do you like the _____?

B. I think (it's / they're) delicious.

A. I'm glad you like (it / them). Would you care for some more?

B. Yes, please. But not (too much / too many). Just (a little / a few).
My doctor says that (too much / too many) _____ (is / are) bad for my health.

chocolate cake

cookies

ice cream

How to Say It!

**Complimenting
About Food**

A. This *chicken* is delicious!*
B. I'm glad you like it.

A. These *potatoes* are delicious!*
B. I'm glad you like them.

* delicious / very good / excellent / wonderful / fantastic

Practice conversations with other students.

TWO BAGS OF GROCERIES

Henry is at the supermarket, and he's really upset. He just bought some groceries, and he can't believe he just spent* sixty dollars! He bought only a few oranges, a few apples, a little milk, a little ice cream, and a few eggs.

He also bought just a little coffee, a few onions, a few bananas, a little rice, a little cheese, and a few lemons. He didn't buy very much fish, he didn't buy very many grapes, and he didn't buy very much meat.

Henry just spent sixty dollars, but he's walking out of the supermarket with only two bags of groceries. No wonder he's upset!

* spend – spent

✔ READING *CHECK-UP*

Q & A

Using these models, make questions and answers based on the story.

A. How many *oranges* did he buy?
B. He bought only a few *oranges*.

A. How much *milk* did he buy?
B. He bought only a little *milk*.

How About You?

What did YOU buy the last time you went to the supermarket?

I bought { a few . . .
           a little . . .

LISTENING

Listen and choose what the people are talking about.

1. a. cake   b. carrots   5. a. eggs   b. butter
2. a. fish   b. potatoes   6. a. rice   b. french fries
3. a. cookies   b. milk   7. a. oranges   b. salad
4. a. cheese   b. meatballs   8. a. lemonade   b. lemons

DELICIOUS!

Lucy likes french fries. In fact, she eats them all the time. Her friends often tell her that she eats too many french fries, but Lucy doesn't think so. She thinks they're delicious.

Fred likes ice cream. In fact, he eats it all the time. His doctor often tells him that he eats too much ice cream, but Fred doesn't think so. He thinks it's delicious.

TASTES TERRIBLE!

Daniel doesn't like vegetables. In fact, he never eats them. His parents often tell him that vegetables are good for him, but Daniel doesn't care. He thinks they taste terrible.

Alice doesn't like yogurt. In fact, she never eats it. Her children often tell her that yogurt is good for her, but Alice doesn't care. She thinks it tastes terrible.

ON YOUR OWN

Tell about foods you like.

What foods do you think are delicious?
How often do you eat them?
Are they good for you, or are they bad for you?

Tell about foods you don't like.

What foods do you think taste terrible?
How often do you eat them?
Are they good for you, or are they bad for you?

Listen. Then say it.	Say it. Then listen.
Let's make a salad for dinner!	Let's make pizza for lunch!
Let's make eggs for breakfast!	Let's have ice cream for dessert!
Would you care for some more cake?	Would you care for some more cookies?
It's bad for my health.	They're bad for my health.

SIDE *by* SIDE JOURNAL

Write in your journal about your favorite foods. What are they? How often do you eat them? Why do you like them?

CHAPTER SUMMARY

GRAMMAR

COUNT / NON-COUNT NOUNS

There isn't any	bread. lettuce. flour.		There aren't any	apples. eggs. lemons.

How much	milk cheese ice cream	do you want?	Not too	much.	Just	a little.
How many	cookies french fries meatballs			many.		a few.

KEY VOCABULARY

FOODS

apple pie	carrots	fish	ketchup	meatballs	oranges	salad	sugar
apples	cheese	flour	lemonade	milk	pears	salt	tea
bananas	chicken	french fries	lemons	mustard	pepper	sandwich	tomatoes
bread	coffee	grapes	lettuce	omelet	pizza	soda	vegetables
butter	cookies	hamburgers	mayonnaise	onions	potatoes	soy sauce	yogurt
cake	eggs	ice cream	meat	orange juice	rice	spaghetti	

3

Partitives
Count/Non-Count Nouns
Imperatives

- Buying Food
- Describing Food
- Eating in a Restaurant
- Recipes

VOCABULARY PREVIEW

1. a **can** of soup
2. a **jar** of jam
3. a **bottle** of ketchup
4. a **box** of cereal
5. a **bag** of flour
6. a **loaf** of white bread
7. two **loaves** of whole wheat bread
8. a **bunch** of bananas
9. a **head** of lettuce
10. a **dozen** eggs
11. a **pint** of ice cream
12. a **quart** of orange juice
13. a **gallon** of milk
14. a **pound** of meat
15. a **half pound**
    half a pound } of cheese

Do We Need Anything from the Supermarket?

My Shopping List

a can of soup
a jar of jam
a bottle of ketchup
a box of cereal
a bag of flour
a loaf of white bread
2 loaves of whole wheat bread
a bunch of bananas
2 bunches of carrots

a head of lettuce
a dozen eggs

a pt.* of ice cream
a qt.* of orange juice
a gal.* of milk
a lb.* of meat
1/2 lb.* of cheese

* pt. = pint
qt. = quart
gal. = gallon
lb. = pound

A. Do we need anything from the supermarket?

B. Yes. We need a loaf of bread.

A. A loaf of bread?

B. Yes.

A. Anything else?

B. No. Just a loaf of bread.

1.　　2.　　3.　　4.　　5.

6.　　7.　　8.　　9.　　10.

Make a Shopping List!

What do you need from the supermarket?
Make a shopping list.

How Much Does a Head of Lettuce Cost?

1¢	$.01	one cent	$1.00	one dollar
25¢	$.25	twenty-five cents	$10.00	ten dollars

A. How much does **a head of lettuce** cost?

B. **A dollar ninety-five.*** ($1.95)

A. A DOLLAR NINETY-FIVE?! That's a lot of money!

B. You're right. **Lettuce** is very expensive this week.

* $1.95 = { a dollar ninety-five
one dollar and ninety-five cents

A. How much does **a pound of apples** cost?

B. **Two eighty-nine.*** ($2.89)

A. TWO EIGHTY-NINE?! That's a lot of money!

B. You're right. **Apples** are very expensive this week.

* $2.89 = { two eighty-nine
two dollars and eighty-nine cents

1.

2.

3.

4.

5.

6.

7.

8.

READING

NOTHING TO EAT FOR DINNER

Joan got home late from work today, and she was very hungry. When she opened the refrigerator, she was upset. There was nothing to eat for dinner. Joan sat down and made a shopping list. She needed a head of lettuce, a bunch of carrots, a quart of milk, a dozen eggs, two pounds of tomatoes, half a pound of chicken, and a loaf of bread.

Joan rushed out of the house and drove to the supermarket. When she got there, she was very disappointed. There wasn't any lettuce. There weren't any carrots. There wasn't any milk. There weren't any eggs. There weren't any tomatoes. There wasn't any chicken, and there wasn't any bread.

Joan was tired and upset. In fact, she was so tired and upset that she lost her appetite, drove home, didn't have dinner, and went to bed.

✔ READING CHECK-UP

Q & A

Joan is at the supermarket. Using these models, create dialogs based on the story.

A. Excuse me. I'm looking for *a head of lettuce.*
B. Sorry. There isn't any more *lettuce.*
A. There isn't?
B. No, there isn't. Sorry.

A. Excuse me. I'm looking for *a bunch of carrots.*
B. Sorry. There aren't any more *carrots.*
A. There aren't?
B. No, there aren't. Sorry.

LISTENING

Listen and choose what the people are talking about.

1. a. chicken   b. milk
2. a. oranges   b. flour
3. a. cookies   b. bread
4. a. potatoes   b. lettuce
5. a. eggs   b. meat
6. a. cereal   b. bananas
7. a. cake   b. soup
8. a. onions   b. soda

What Would You Like?

A. What would you like **for dessert**?

B. I can't decide. What do you recommend?

A. I recommend our **chocolate ice cream**. Everybody says **it's** delicious.*

B. Okay. Please give me **a dish of chocolate ice cream**.

A. What would you like **for breakfast**?

B. I can't decide. What do you recommend?

A. I recommend our **scrambled eggs**. Everybody says **they're** out of this world.*

B. Okay. Please give me **an order of scrambled eggs**.

* delicious / very good / excellent / wonderful / fantastic / magnificent / out of this world

1. for lunch?
a bowl of

2. for breakfast?
an order of

3. for dessert?
a piece of

4. to drink?
a glass of

5. for dessert?
a bowl of

6. to drink?
a cup of

7. for dessert?
a dish of

8.

How to Say It!

Making a Recommendation About Food

A. What do you recommend for *breakfast*?*

B. I $\left\{ \begin{array}{l} \text{recommend} \\ \text{suggest} \end{array} \right\}$ the *pancakes*.

* breakfast / lunch / dinner / dessert

Practice conversations with other students. Ask for and make recommendations.

Stanley's Favorite Recipes

Are you going to have a party soon? Do you want to cook something special? Stanley the chef recommends this recipe for VEGETABLE STEW. Everybody says it's fantastic!

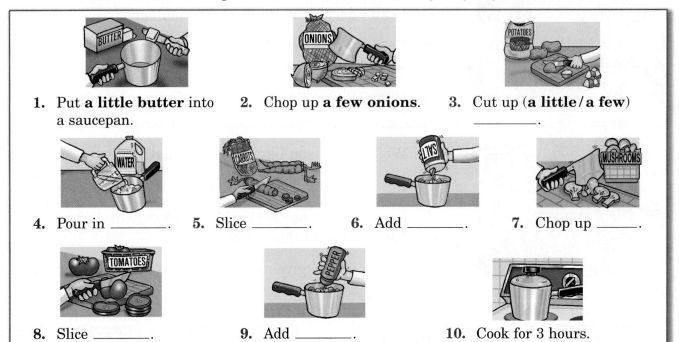

1. Put **a little butter** into a saucepan.
2. Chop up **a few onions**.
3. Cut up (**a little / a few**) _____.

4. Pour in _____.
5. Slice _____.
6. Add _____.
7. Chop up _____.

8. Slice _____.
9. Add _____.
10. Cook for 3 hours.

When is your English teacher's birthday? Do you want to bake a special cake? Stanley the chef recommends this recipe for FRUITCAKE. Everybody says it's out of this world!

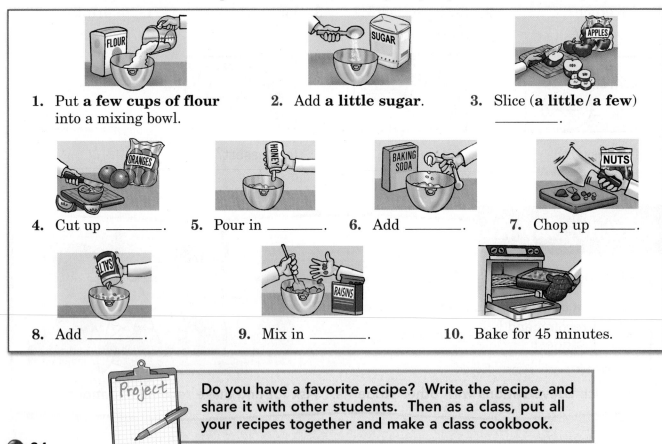

1. Put **a few cups of flour** into a mixing bowl.
2. Add **a little sugar**.
3. Slice (**a little / a few**) _____.

4. Cut up _____.
5. Pour in _____.
6. Add _____.
7. Chop up _____.

8. Add _____.
9. Mix in _____.
10. Bake for 45 minutes.

Project

Do you have a favorite recipe? Write the recipe, and share it with other students. Then as a class, put all your recipes together and make a class cookbook.

READING

AT THE CONTINENTAL RESTAURANT

Yesterday was Sherman and Dorothy Johnson's thirty-fifth wedding anniversary. They went to the Continental Restaurant for dinner. This restaurant is a very special place for Sherman and Dorothy because they went there on their first date thirty-six years ago.

Sherman and Dorothy sat at a quiet romantic table in the corner. They looked at the menu, and then they ordered dinner. For an appetizer, Dorothy ordered a bowl of vegetable soup, and Sherman ordered a glass of tomato juice. For the main course, Dorothy ordered baked chicken with rice, and Sherman ordered broiled fish with potatoes. For dessert, Dorothy ordered a piece of apple pie, and Sherman ordered a bowl of strawberries.

Sherman and Dorothy enjoyed their dinner very much. The soup was delicious, and the tomato juice was fresh. The chicken was wonderful, and the rice was tasty. The fish was fantastic, and the potatoes were excellent. The apple pie was magnificent, and the strawberries were out of this world.

Sherman and Dorothy had a wonderful evening at the Continental Restaurant. It was a very special anniversary.

ROLE PLAY

Sherman and Dorothy are ordering dinner from their waiter or waitress. Using these lines to begin, work in groups of three and create a role play based on the story.

   A. Would you like to order now?
   B. Yes. For an appetizer, I'd like . . .
   C. And I'd like . . .

Now, the waiter or waitress is asking about the dinner. Using this model, continue your role play based on all the foods in the story.

   A. How (is / are) the _____?
   B. (It's / They're) _____.
   A. I'm glad you like (it / them).
         And how (is / are) the _____?
   C. (It's / They're) _____.
   A. I'm glad you like (it / them).

25

Listen. Then say it.	Say it. Then listen.
a bowl of soup	a glass of milk
a head of lettuce	a jar of jam
a piece of apple pie	a pound of oranges
a bag of onions	a dish of ice cream

In your journal, write about a special meal you enjoyed—in your home, in someone else's home, or at a restaurant. What foods did you have? Who was at the meal? Why was it special?

CHAPTER SUMMARY

GRAMMAR

COUNT / NON-COUNT NOUNS

Lettuce Butter Milk	is	very expensive.
Apples Carrots Onions	are	

Add	a little	salt. sugar. honey.
	a few	potatoes. nuts. raisins.

I recommend our	chocolate ice cream. scrambled eggs.

It's They're	delicious.

IMPERATIVES

Please **give me** a dish of ice cream.
Put a little butter into a saucepan.
Cook for 3 hours.

PARTITIVES

a bag of flour	**a dozen** eggs	**a jar of** jam	**a bowl of** chicken soup
a bottle of ketchup	**a gallon of** milk	**a loaf of** bread	**a cup of** hot chocolate
a box of cereal	**a half pound (half a pound) of** cheese	**a pint of** ice cream	**a dish of** ice cream
a bunch of bananas		**a pound of** meat	**a glass of** milk
a can of soup	**a head of** lettuce	**a quart of** orange juice	**an order of** scrambled eggs
			a piece of apple pie

KEY VOCABULARY

FOOD ITEMS

apple pie	hot chocolate	scrambled eggs	tomato juice	
baked chicken	jam	soup	vanilla ice cream	
baking soda	mushrooms	chicken soup	water	
broiled fish	nuts	vegetable soup	white bread	
chocolate ice cream	pancakes	strawberries	whole wheat bread	
honey	raisins	Swiss cheese		

DESCRIBING FOOD

delicious
excellent
fantastic
magnificent
out of this world
very good
wonderful

SIDE by SIDE Gazette

Volume 2   Number 1

Food Shopping

Everybody eats, and everybody shops for food!

In the past, people shopped for fruits, vegetables, bread, and meat at small food stores and at open markets. Before there were refrigerators, it was difficult to keep food fresh for a long time, so people shopped almost every day.

Life today is very different from the past. Refrigerators keep food fresh so people don't have to shop every day. People also have very busy lives. They have time to shop for food only once or twice a week.

People shop for food in different kinds of places—in small grocery stores, at large supermarkets, and sometimes at enormous wholesale stores that sell food and other items at very low prices. Some people even shop on the Internet. They order food online, and the company delivers it to their home. And in many places around the world, people still shop in little food stores and at open markets. There are certainly many different ways to shop for food these days!

FACT FILE

One Day's Food

Eggs: The world's hens produce more than 2 billion eggs a day—enough eggs to make an omelet the size of the island of Cyprus!

Chocolate: The world produces 8,818 tons of cocoa beans every day—enough to make 700 million chocolate bars!

Rice: The world produces 1.6 million tons of rice every day—an amount the size of Egypt's Great Pyramid!

I'd like _____ , please.

- a hamburger
- a hot dog
- a sandwich
- a taco
- a bowl of chili
- a slice of pizza
- a donut
- a bagel
- a muffin

AROUND THE WORLD

Where People Shop for Food

People in different places shop for food in different ways.

These people shop for food at an open market.

This person buys a fresh loaf of bread every day at this bakery.

These people go to a big supermarket once a week.

Where do people shop for food in countries you know? Where do YOU shop for food?

Send a message to a keypal. Tell about the meals you eat.

LISTENING

Attention, Food Shoppers!

_d_	**1**	cereal	**a.**	$2.75
___	**2**	bread	**b.**	$ .40
___	**3**	orange juice	**c.**	$3.25
___	**4**	ice cream	**d.**	$3.49
___	**5**	bananas	**e.**	$1.79

What Are They Saying?

4

Future Tense: Will
Time Expressions
Might

- **Telling About the Future**
- **Probability**
- **Possibility**
- **Warnings**

VOCABULARY PREVIEW

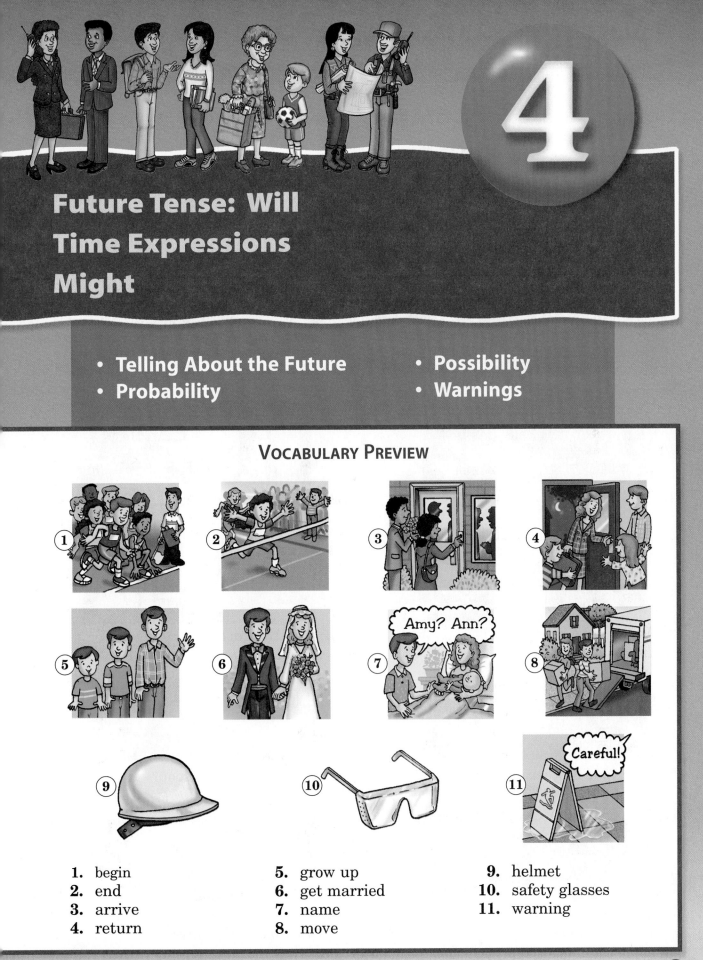

1. begin
2. end
3. arrive
4. return
5. grow up
6. get married
7. name
8. move
9. helmet
10. safety glasses
11. warning

Will the Train Arrive Soon?

(I will)	I'll
(He will)	He'll
(She will)	She'll
(It will)	It'll
(We will)	We'll
(You will)	You'll
(They will)	They'll

} work.

Will he work?
Yes, he will.

A. Will the train arrive soon?

B. Yes, it will. It'll arrive in five minutes.

1. Will the game begin soon?
at 7:00

2. Will Ms. Lopez return soon?
in an hour

3. Will you be ready soon?
in a few minutes

4. Will the guests be here soon?
in half an hour

5. Will your brother get home soon?
in a little while

6. Will you be back soon?
in a week

7. Will the storm end soon?
in a few hours

8. Will I get out of the hospital soon?
in two or three days

What Do You Think?

I He She It We You They	will work.

I He She It We You They	won't work. (will not)

Do you think it'll rain tomorrow?

Maybe it will, and maybe it won't. We'll just have to wait and see.

1. Do you think Mr. Lee will give us a test tomorrow?

2. Do you think your daughter will get married soon?

3. Do you think your parents will move to Florida?

4. Do you think it'll be very cold this winter?

5. Do you think we'll have to work this weekend?

6. Do you think you'll be happy in your new neighborhood?

7. Do you think I'll be famous some day?

8. Do you think there will be many people at the beach tomorrow?

9. Do you think _____?

31

I CAN'T WAIT FOR SPRING TO COME!

I'm tired of winter. I'm tired of snow, I'm tired of cold weather, and I'm sick and tired of winter coats and boots! Just think! In a few more weeks it won't be winter any more. It'll be spring. The weather won't be cold. It'll be warm. It won't snow any more. It'll be sunny. I won't have to stay indoors any more. I'll go outside and play with my friends. We'll ride bicycles and play baseball again.

In a few more weeks our neighborhood won't look sad and gray any more. The flowers will bloom, and the trees will become green again. My family will spend more time outdoors. My father will work in the yard. He'll cut the grass and paint the fence. My mother will work in the yard, too. She'll buy new flowers and plant them in the garden. On weekends we won't just sit in the living room and watch TV. We'll go for walks in the park, and we'll have picnics on Sunday afternoons.

I can't wait for spring to come! Hurry, spring!

✔ READING CHECK-UP

TRUE, FALSE, OR MAYBE?

Answer True, False, or Maybe (if the answer isn't in the story).

1. It's spring.
2. The boy in the story likes to go outside during the spring.
3. The boy has a cold.
4. The trees are green now.
5. The park is near their house.
6. The boy plays baseball with his friends all year.
7. The family has a TV in their living room.
8. The boy's family doesn't like winter.

How About You?

What's your favorite season—spring? summer? fall? winter? Why? What's the weather like in your favorite season? What do you like to do?

They Really Can't Decide

| I |
| He |
| She |
| It | $\Big\}$ might clean it today.
| We |
| You |
| They |

A. When are you going to clean your apartment?

B. I don't know. I might clean it today, or I might clean it next Saturday. I really can't decide.

A. Where are you going to go for your vacation?

B. We don't know. We might go to Mexico, or we might go to Japan. We really can't decide.

1. What's he going to make for dinner tonight?

2. What color is she going to paint her bedroom?

3. What are they going to name their new daughter?

4. When are you two going to get married?

5. What are you going to buy your brother for his birthday?

6. What are they going to do tonight?

7. How are you going to get to school tomorrow?

8. What's he going to name his new puppy?

9. What are you going to be when you grow up?

Careful!

A. Careful! Put on your helmet!

B. I'm sorry. What did you say?

A. Put on your helmet! You might hurt your head.

B. Oh. Thanks for the warning.

1. Put on your safety glasses!
   hurt your eyes

2. Don't stand there!
   get hit

3. Watch your step!
   fall

4. Don't touch that machine!
   get hurt

5. Don't touch those wires!
   get a shock

6.

How to Say It!

Asking for Repetition

A. *Careful! Watch your step!*

B. *I'm sorry.* { What did you say?
   Could you please repeat that?
   Could you say that again? }

Practice some conversations on this page again. Ask for repetition in different ways.

I'm Afraid I Might Drown

A. Would you like to go swimming with me?

B. No, I don't think so.

A. Why not?

B. I'm afraid I might drown.

A. Don't worry! You won't drown.

B. Are you sure?

A. I'm positive!

B. Okay. I'll go swimming with you.

1. *go skiing*
break my leg

2. *go to the beach*
get a sunburn

3. *go dancing*
step on your feet

4. *take a walk in the park*
catch a cold

5. *go to the movies*
fall asleep

6. *go to the company picnic*
have a terrible time

7. *go on the roller coaster*
get sick

8. *go sailing*
get seasick

9.

JUST IN CASE

Larry didn't go to work today, and he might not go to work tomorrow either. He might see his doctor instead. He's feeling absolutely terrible, and he thinks he might have the flu. Larry isn't positive, but he doesn't want to take any chances. He thinks it might be a good idea for him to see his doctor . . . just in case.

Mrs. Randall didn't go to the office today, and she might not go to the office tomorrow either. She might go to the doctor instead. She feels nauseous every morning, and she thinks she might be pregnant. Mrs. Randall isn't positive, but she doesn't want to take any chances. She thinks it might be a good idea for her to go to the doctor . . . just in case.

Tommy and Julie Harris didn't go to school today, and they might not go to school tomorrow either. They might stay home in bed instead. They have little red spots all over their arms and legs. Mr. and Mrs. Harris think their children might have the measles. They aren't positive, but they don't want to take any chances. They think it might be a good idea for Tommy and Julie to stay home in bed . . . just in case.

✓ READING *CHECK-UP*

CHOOSE

Larry is "calling in sick." Choose the correct words and then practice the conversation.

A. Hello. This is Larry Parker. I'm afraid I (might   can't)[1] come to work today. I think I (will   might)[2] have the flu.

B. That's too bad. (Are you   Will you)[3] going to see your doctor?

A. I think I (might   sure).[4]

B. (Not   Will)[5] you be at work tomorrow?

A. I'm not sure. I (might not   might)[6] go to work tomorrow either.

B. Well, I hope you feel better soon.

A. Thank you.

LISTENING

WHAT'S THE LINE?

Mrs. Harris (from the story on page 36) is calling Tommy and Julie's school. Listen and choose the correct lines.

1. a. Hello. This is Mrs. Harris.
   b. Hello. This is the Park Elementary School.
2. a. I can't.
   b. Tommy and Julie won't be in school today.
3. a. They might have the measles.
   b. Yes. This is their mother.
4. a. They aren't bad. They're just sick.
   b. Yes.
5. a. Thank you.
   b. It might be a good idea.

> Good morning.
> Park Elementary School.

WHAT'S THE WORD?

Listen and choose the word you hear.

1. a. can't   b. might
2. a. want to   b. won't
3. a. here   b. there
4. a. we'll   b. will
5. a. they'll   b. they
6. a. hurt   b. hit
7. a. I   b. I'll
8. a. red   b. wet
9. a. sick   b. seasick

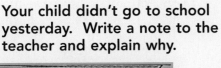

Write a Note!

Your child didn't go to school yesterday. Write a note to the teacher and explain why.

.............., 20.......

Dear ....,

.... didn't go to school yesterday because

....

....

Sincerely,

....

PRONUNCIATION *Going to*

going to = gonna

Listen. Then say it.

When are you going to
 clean your room?

What color is she going to
 paint her bedroom?

How are they going to get
 to school?

Say it. Then listen.

When are you going to
 get married?

What's he going to name
 his cat?

When am I going to get
 out of the hospital?

SIDE by SIDE JOURNAL

Write in your journal about your future. Where do you think you might live? Where do you think you might work? What do you think might happen in your life?

GRAMMAR

FUTURE TENSE: WILL

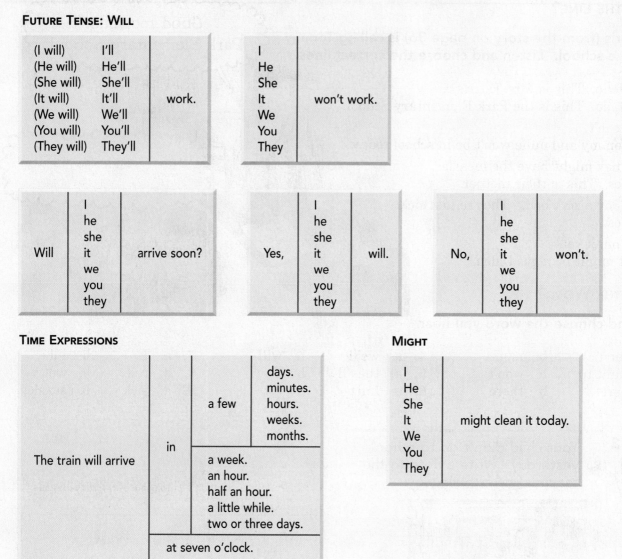

(I will)	I'll
(He will)	He'll
(She will)	She'll
(It will)	It'll
(We will)	We'll
(You will)	You'll
(They will)	They'll

work.

| I / He / She / It / We / You / They | won't work. |

Will [I he she it we you they] arrive soon?

Yes, [I he she it we you they] will.

No, [I he she it we you they] won't.

TIME EXPRESSIONS

The train will arrive in a few — days. minutes. hours. weeks. months.

in — a week. an hour. half an hour. a little while. two or three days.

at seven o'clock.

MIGHT

I / He / She / It / We / You / They might clean it today.

KEY VOCABULARY

BEGINNINGS & ENDINGS
arrive
be back
begin
end
get home
return

HEALTH
catch a cold
get a sunburn
get seasick
get sick

the flu
the measles

INJURIES
break *my* leg
fall
get a shock
get hit
get hurt
hurt *your* head/eyes

LIFE EVENTS
get married
grow up
move
name (v)

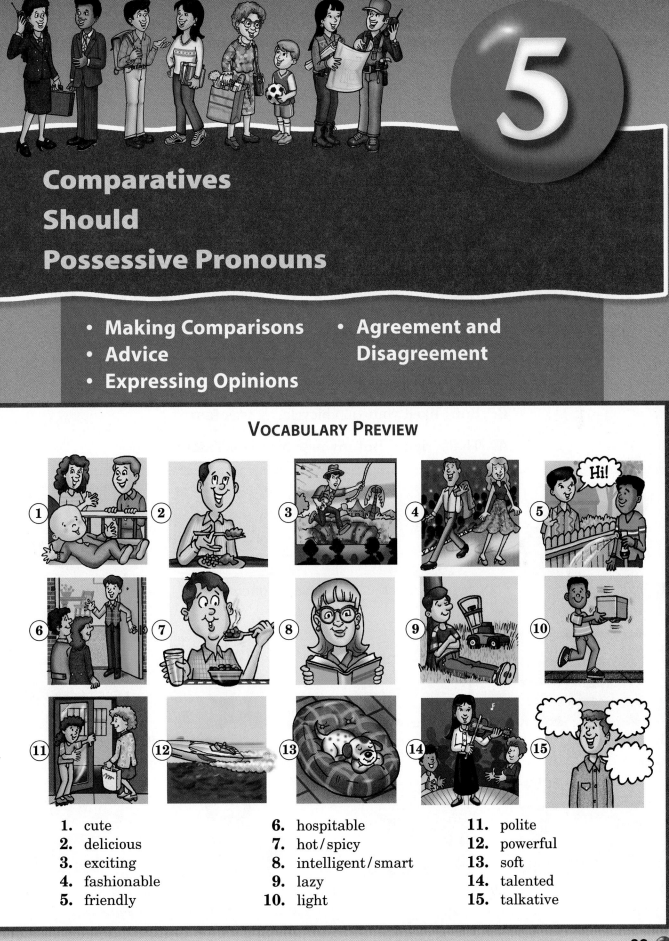

Comparatives
Should
Possessive Pronouns

- **Making Comparisons**
- **Advice**
- **Expressing Opinions**
- **Agreement and Disagreement**

VOCABULARY PREVIEW

1. cute
2. delicious
3. exciting
4. fashionable
5. friendly
6. hospitable
7. hot / spicy
8. intelligent / smart
9. lazy
10. light
11. polite
12. powerful
13. soft
14. talented
15. talkative

My New Bicycle Is Faster

soft – softer small – smaller	large – larger safe – safer	big – bigger hot – hotter	fancy – fancier pretty – prettier

A. I think you'll like my new bicycle.

B. But I liked your OLD bicycle. It was **fast**.

A. That's right. But my new bicycle is **faster**.

1. rug
soft

2. tennis racket
light

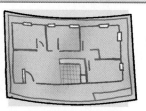

3. apartment
large

4. neighborhood
safe

5. office
big

6. recipe for chili
hot

7. dog
friendly

8. sports car
fancy

9. dishwasher
quiet

10. wig
pretty

11. cell phone
small

12. cat
cute

My New Rocking Chair Is More Comfortable

fast – faster	comfortable – more comfortable
nice – nicer	beautiful – more beautiful
big – bigger	interesting – more interesting
pretty – prettier	intelligent – more intelligent

A. I think you'll like my new rocking chair.

B. But I liked your OLD rocking chair. It was **comfortable**.

A. That's right. But my new rocking chair is **more comfortable**.

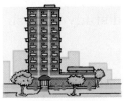

1. *apartment building*
   beautiful

2. *roommate*
   interesting

3. *girlfriend*
   intelligent

4. *boyfriend*
   handsome

5. *briefcase*
   attractive

6. *computer*
   powerful

7. *printer*
   fast

8. *English teacher*
   smart

9. *recipe for meatloaf*
   delicious

10. *boss*
    nice

11. *parrot*
    talkative

12.

Bicycles Are Safer Than Motorcycles

I
He
She
It
We
You
They
} should study.

Should I study?

A. Should I buy a bicycle or a motorcycle?

B. I think you should buy a bicycle.

A. Why?

B. Bicycles are **safer than** motorcycles.

safe

A. Should he study English or Latin?

B. I think he should study English.

A. Why?

B. English is **more useful than** Latin.

useful

cheap

1. Should I buy a used car or a new car?

Ellen interesting   Helen

2. Should he go out with Ellen or Helen?

friendly

3. Should she buy a dog or a cat?

honest

4. Should I vote for Linda Lee or Gary Green?

5. Should she take a course with Professor Blake or Professor Drake?

6. Should they plant flowers or vegetables this spring?

7. Should we buy this fan or that fan?

8. Should she buy these earrings or those earrings?

9. Should he take piano lessons with Mrs. Clark or Miss Smith?

10. Should I buy the hat in my left hand or the hat in my right hand?

11. Should she buy fur gloves or leather gloves?

12. Should I buy a notebook computer or a desktop computer?

13. Should I hire Ms. Parker or Ms. Jones?

14. Should I fire Mr. Mason or Mr. Grimes?

15. Should we rent this movie or that movie?

16.

43

READING

IT ISN'T EASY BEING A TEENAGER

I try to be a good son, but no matter how hard I try, my parents never seem to be satisfied. They think I should be a better* son. They think I should eat healthier food, I should wear nicer clothes, and I should get better grades. And according to them, my hair should be shorter, my room should be neater, and my friends should be more polite when they come to visit.

You know . . . it isn't easy being a teenager.

IT ISN'T EASY BEING PARENTS

We try to be good parents, but no matter how hard we try, our children never seem to be satisfied. They think we should be better parents. They think we should wear more fashionable clothes, we should drive a newer car, and we should listen to more interesting music. And according to them, we should be more sympathetic when they talk about their problems, we should be friendlier when their friends come to visit, and we should be more understanding when they come home late on Saturday night.

You know . . . it isn't easy being parents.

* good – better

✔ READING CHECK-UP

WHAT'S THE WORD?

According to this boy's parents, he doesn't eat __healthy__ ¹ food, he doesn't wear _____ ² clothes, he doesn't get _____ ³ grades, his hair isn't _____ ⁴, and his friends aren't _____ ⁵ when they come to visit.

According to their children, these parents don't wear _____ ⁶ clothes, they don't have a _____ ⁷ car, they don't listen to _____ ⁸ music, and they aren't _____ ⁹ when their children's friends come to visit.

LISTENING

Listen and choose what the people are talking about.

1. a. TV   b. printer
2. a. chair   b. recipe
3. a. hair   b. apartment

4. a. offices   b. friends
5. a. neighborhood   b. briefcase
6. a. rug   b. computer

Don't Be Ridiculous!

my – mine	our – ours
his – his	your – yours
her – hers	their – theirs

A. You know, my dog isn't as friendly as your dog.

B. Don't be ridiculous! Yours is MUCH friendlier than **mine**.

A. You know, my novels aren't as interesting as Ernest Hemingway's novels.

B. Don't be ridiculous! Yours are MUCH more interesting than **his**.

 clean

1. *my apartment*
your apartment

 powerful

2. *my computer*
Bob's computer

 nice

3. *my boss*
your boss

 comfortable

4. *my furniture*
your furniture

 big

5. *my house*
the Jacksons' house

 She sells sea shells... good

6. *my pronunciation*
Maria's pronunciation

pretty

7. *my garden*
your garden

 FRUITCAKE delicious

8. *my recipe for fruitcake*
Stanley's recipe for fruitcake

9.

BROWNSVILLE

The Taylor family lived in Brownsville for many years. And for many years, Brownsville was a very good place to live. The streets were clean, the parks were safe, the bus system was reliable, and the schools were good.

But Brownsville changed. Today the streets aren't as clean as they used to be. The parks aren't as safe as they used to be. The bus system isn't as reliable as it used to be. And the schools aren't as good as they used to be.

Because of the changes in Brownsville, the Taylor family moved to Newport last year. In Newport the streets are cleaner, the parks are safer, the bus system is more reliable, and the schools are better. The Taylors are happy in Newport, but they were happier in Brownsville. Although Newport has cleaner streets, safer parks, a more reliable bus system, and better schools, Brownsville has friendlier people. They're nicer, more polite, and more hospitable than the people in Newport.

The Taylors miss Brownsville. Even though they're now living in Newport, Brownsville will always be their real home.

✔ READING *CHECK-UP*

Q & A

The people of Brownsville are calling Mayor Brown's radio talk show. They're upset about Brownsville's streets, parks, bus system, and schools. Using this model and the story, call Mayor Brown.

A. This is Mayor Brown. You're on the air.
B. Mayor Brown, I'm very upset about the *streets* here in Brownsville.
A. Why do you say that?
B. *They aren't* as *clean* as *they* used to be.
A. Do you really think so?
B. Definitely! You know . . . they say the *streets* in Newport *are cleaner*.
A. I'll see what I can do. Thank you for calling.

ON THE AIR

How to Say It!

Agreeing & Disagreeing

A.
{
I think . . .
In my opinion, . . .
}

B.
{
I agree.
I agree with you.
I think so, too.
}

C.
{
I disagree.
I disagree with you.
I don't think so.
}

Practice interactions on this page, using these expressions for agreeing and disagreeing.

INTERACTIONS

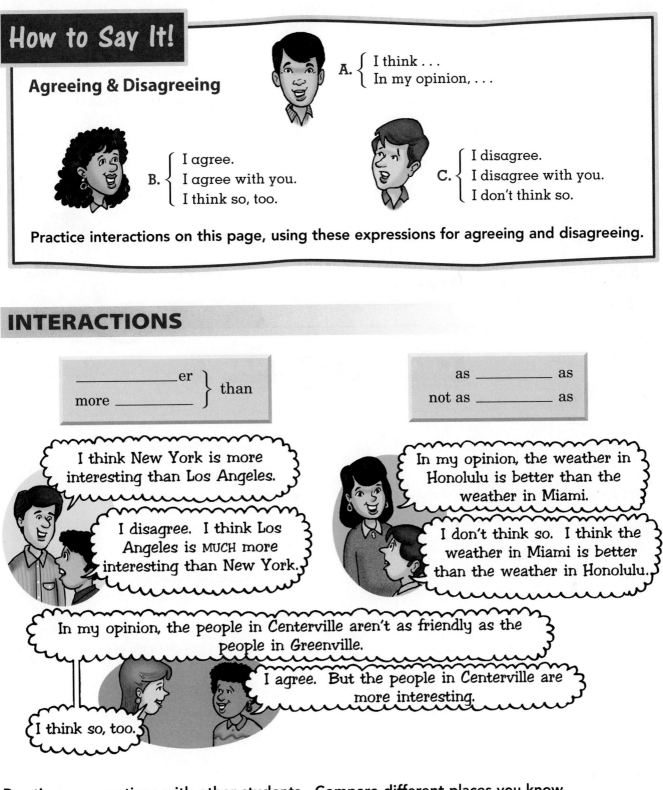

_____er
more _____
} than

as _____ as
not as _____ as

I think New York is more interesting than Los Angeles.

I disagree. I think Los Angeles is MUCH more interesting than New York.

In my opinion, the weather in Honolulu is better than the weather in Miami.

I don't think so. I think the weather in Miami is better than the weather in Honolulu.

In my opinion, the people in Centerville aren't as friendly as the people in Greenville.

I agree. But the people in Centerville are more interesting.

I think so, too.

Practice conversations with other students. Compare different places you know.
Talk about . . .

the streets (*quiet, safe, clean, wide, busy*)
the buildings (*tall, modern, attractive*)
the weather (*cold, cool, warm, hot, rainy, snowy*)
the people (*friendly, nice, polite, honest, happy, hospitable, talkative, healthy*)
the city in general (*large, interesting, exciting, expensive*)

PRONUNCIATION Yes / No Questions with *or*

Listen. Then say it.

Should I buy a bicycle or a motorcycle?

Should we buy this fan or that fan?

Should he go out with Ellen or Helen?

Should she buy fur gloves or leather gloves?

Say it. Then listen.

Should they plant flowers or vegetables?

Should she buy these earrings or those earrings?

Should I hire Ms. Carter or Mr. Price?

Should I buy a notebook computer or a desktop computer?

SIDE by SIDE JOURNAL

In your journal, compare your home town and the place you live now. Or compare any two places you know.

CHAPTER SUMMARY

GRAMMAR

COMPARATIVES

My new apartment is	colder larger bigger prettier	than my old apartment.
	more comfortable more attractive	

SHOULD

Should	I he she it we you they	study?

I He She It We You They	should study.

POSSESSIVE PRONOUNS

This dog is much friendlier than	mine. his. hers. ours. yours. theirs.

KEY VOCABULARY

DESCRIBING

attractive	comfortable	fashionable	hospitable	neat	reliable	sympathetic
beautiful	convenient	fast	hot	new	safe	talented
big	cool	friendly	intelligent	nice	short	talkative
busy	cute	good–better	interesting	polite	small	tall
capable	delicious	handsome	large	powerful	smart	understanding
cheap	exciting	happy	lazy	pretty	snowy	useful
clean	expensive	healthy	light	quiet	soft	warm
cold	fancy	honest	modern	rainy	spicy	wide

Superlatives

- **Describing People, Places, and Things**
- **Shopping in a Department Store**
- **Expressing Opinions**

VOCABULARY PREVIEW

1. energetic
2. funny
3. generous
4. helpful
5. honest
6. lazy
7. mean
8. nice
9. noisy
10. obnoxious
11. patient
12. popular
13. rude
14. sloppy
15. stubborn

49

The Smartest Person I Know

smart – the smartest kind – the kindest	nice – the nicest safe – the safest
funny – the funniest pretty – the prettiest	big – the biggest hot – the hottest

A. I think your friend Margaret is very **smart**.

B. She certainly is. She's **the smartest** person I know.

1. *your Aunt Emma*
kind

2. *your friend Jim*
bright

3. *your parents*
nice

4. *your Uncle Ted*
funny

5. *your sister*
pretty

6. *your cousin Amy*
friendly

7. *Larry*
lazy

8. *your landlord*
mean

9. *your roommates*
sloppy

The Most Energetic Person I Know

smart – the smartest	energetic – the most energetic
funny – the funniest	interesting – the most interesting
nice – the nicest	patient – the most patient
big – the biggest	stubborn – the most stubborn

A. I think your grandmother is very **energetic**.

B. She certainly is. She's **the most energetic** person I know.

1. *your friend Carlos interesting*

2. *your grandfather generous*

3. *your cousins talented*

4. *our English teacher patient*

5. *your nephew Andrew stubborn*

6. *your younger brother polite*

7. *your older sister bright*

8. *your upstairs neighbor noisy*

9. *your downstairs neighbor rude*

10. *Senator Smith honest*

11. *our history professor boring*

12.

THE NICEST PERSON

| friendly | polite | smart | talented | pretty |

Mr. and Mrs. Jackson are very proud of their daughter, Linda. She's a very nice person. She's friendly, she's polite, she's smart, and she's talented. She's also very pretty.

Mr. and Mrs. Jackson's friends and neighbors always compliment them about Linda. They say she's the nicest person they know. According to them, she's the friendliest, the most polite, the smartest, and the most talented girl in the neighborhood. They also think she's the prettiest.

Mr. and Mrs. Jackson agree. They think Linda is a wonderful girl, and they're proud to say she's their daughter.

THE MOST OBNOXIOUS DOG

| noisy | stubborn | lazy | mean | ugly |

Mr. and Mrs. Hubbard are very embarrassed by their dog, Rex. He's a very obnoxious dog. He's noisy, he's stubborn, he's lazy, and he's mean. He's also very ugly.

Mr. and Mrs. Hubbard's friends and neighbors always complain about Rex. They say he's the most obnoxious dog they know. According to them, he's the noisiest, the most stubborn, the laziest, and the meanest dog in the neighborhood. They also think he's the ugliest.

Mr. and Mrs. Hubbard agree. They think Rex is a horrible dog, and they're ashamed to say he's theirs.

✔ READING *CHECK-UP*

CHOOSE

1. Linda is the (most polite   smart) person I know.
2. She's the most (talented   friendliest) girl in the neighborhood.
3. She's a very (nicest   nice) person.
4. Rex is the most (stubborn   mean) dog in the neighborhood.
5. He's the (lazy   noisiest) dog I know.
6. He's also the most (ugliest   obnoxious) dog in town.

Q & A

The neighbors are talking. Using these models, create dialogs based on the stories.

A. You know . . . I think Linda is very *nice*.
B. I agree. She's the *nicest* girl in the neighborhood.

A. You know . . . I think Rex is very *obnoxious*.
B. You're right. He's the *most obnoxious* dog in the neighborhood.

How About You?

Tell about the nicest person you know.

How to Say It!

Expressing an Opinion

A. { In my opinion, . . .
    As far as I'm concerned, . . .
    If you ask me, . . . }
Linda is the most talented student in our school.

B. I agree. / I disagree.

Practice conversations with other students. Share opinions.

LISTENING

Listen to the sentence. Is the person saying something good or something bad about someone else?

1. a. good   b. bad
2. a. good   b. bad
3. a. good   b. bad
4. a. good   b. bad
5. a. good   b. bad
6. a. good   b. bad
7. a. good   b. bad
8. a. good   b. bad
9. a. good   b. bad

PRONUNCIATION   *Linking Words with Duplicated Consonants*

Listen. Then say it.

She's the nicest teacher in our school.

He's the most stubborn neighbor on our street.

They're the most talented dancers in the world.

Say it. Then listen.

He's the most generous student in our class.

This is the cheapest toothpaste in the store.

He's the most polite taxi driver in the city.

I Want to Buy a Small Radio

a small radio	a comfortable chair	a good car
a smaller radio	a more comfortable chair	a better car
the smallest radio	the most comfortable chair	the best car

A. May I help you?

B. Yes, please. I want to buy a **small** radio.

A. I think you'll like this one. It's VERY **small**.

B. Don't you have a **smaller** one?

A. No, I'm afraid not. This is **the smallest** one we have.

B. Thank you anyway.

A. Sorry we can't help you. Please come again.

A. May I help you?

B. Yes, please. I want to buy a/an _____ _____.

A. I think you'll like this one. It's VERY _____.

B. Don't you have a/an { _____er / more _____ } one?

A. No, I'm afraid not. This is the { _____est / most _____ } one we have.

B. Thank you anyway.

A. Sorry we can't help you. Please come again.

1. *large TV*

2. *comfortable rocking chair*

3. *good CD player*

4. *cheap watch*

5. *fast printer*

6. *elegant evening gown*

7. *small cell phone*

8. *lightweight video camera*

9. *powerful computer*

10. *tall bookcase*

11. *short novel*

12.

BOB'S BARGAIN DEPARTMENT STORE

Bob's Bargain Department Store is the cheapest store in town. However, even though it's the cheapest, it isn't the most popular. People don't shop there very often because the products are bad.* In fact, some people say the products there are the worst in town.

The furniture isn't very comfortable, the clothes aren't very fashionable, the appliances aren't very dependable, and the home entertainment products aren't very good. Besides that, the location isn't very convenient, and the salespeople aren't very helpful.

That's why people don't shop at Bob's Bargain Department Store very often, even though it's the cheapest store in town.

THE LORD AND LADY DEPARTMENT STORE

The Lord and Lady Department Store sells very good products. In fact, some people say the products there are the best in town.

They sell the most comfortable furniture, the most fashionable clothes, the most dependable appliances, and the best home entertainment products. And besides that, their location is the most convenient, and their salespeople are the most helpful in town.

However, even though the Lord and Lady Department Store is the best store in town, people don't shop there very often because it's also the most expensive.

* bad – worse – worst

THE SUPER SAVER DEPARTMENT STORE

The Super Saver Department Store is the most popular store in town. It isn't the cheapest, and it isn't the most expensive. It doesn't have the best products, and it doesn't have the worst.

The furniture isn't the most comfortable you can buy, but it's more comfortable than the furniture at many other stores. The clothes aren't the most fashionable you can buy, but they're more fashionable than the clothes at many other stores. The appliances aren't the most dependable you can buy, but they're more dependable than the appliances at many other stores. The home entertainment products aren't the best you can buy, but they're better than the home entertainment products at many other stores. In addition, the location is convenient, and the salespeople are helpful.

You can see why the Super Saver Department Store is the most popular store in town. The prices are reasonable, and the products are good. That's why people like to shop there.

✔ READING *CHECK-UP*

TRUE OR FALSE?

1. Bob's Bargain Department Store is the most popular store in town.
2. The salespeople at Lord and Lady are more helpful than the salespeople at Super Saver.
3. The location of Lord and Lady isn't as convenient as the location of Bob's.
4. The Super Saver Department Store has the best prices in town.
5. The home entertainment products at Super Saver are better than the home entertainment products at Bob's.
6. People in this town say the cheapest department store is the best.

How About You?

Tell about places to shop where you live: the cheapest, the most expensive, the most popular. Tell about the products they sell.

INTERACTIONS *Sharing Opinions*

Practice conversations with other students. Share opinions, and give reasons for your opinions.

In your opinion, . . .

1. Who is the most popular actor/actress in your country?
    Who is the most popular TV star? the best singer?

2. What is the most popular car in your country? the most
    popular sport? the best newspaper? the most popular
    magazine? the best TV program? the most popular food?

3. What is the best city in your country? What is the worst
    city? Why? What are the most interesting tourist sights in
    your country? What are the most popular vacation places?

4. Who is the most important person in your country now?
    Why? Who was the most important person in the history
    of your country? Why?

SIDE *by* SIDE JOURNAL

Who is the most important
person in your life? Why?
Write about this person in
your journal.

CHAPTER SUMMARY

GRAMMAR

SUPERLATIVES

| He's | the smartest
the nicest
the biggest
the busiest | person I know. |
| | the most talented
the most interesting | |

KEY VOCABULARY

DESCRIBING

bad–worse–worst	elegant	good–better–best	lazy	patient	sloppy
boring	energetic	helpful	lightweight	polite	small
bright	fashionable	honest	long	popular	smart
cheap	fast	horrible	mean	powerful	stubborn
comfortable	friendly	interesting	nice	pretty	talented
convenient	funny	kind	noisy	rude	ugly
dependable	generous	large	obnoxious	short	wonderful

Did You Know?

The longest car in the world is 100 feet long. It has 26 wheels, a swimming pool, and a waterbed!

The world's biggest costume party is the Carnival celebration in Brazil. Every day during Carnival, more than 50,000 people walk through the streets in costumes.

The largest subway station in the world is Grand Central Terminal in New York City. Every day more than half a million people pass through the station.

The biggest igloo in the world is the Ice Hotel in Sweden. It has rooms for 150 guests. Every year workers have to rebuild the hotel because it melts in the spring!

FACT FILE

World Geography Facts

- The longest river in the world is the Nile. It is 4,180 miles (6,690 kilometers) long.

- The highest mountain in the world is Mount Everest. It is 29,028 feet (8,848 meters) high.

- The largest ocean in the world is the Pacific Ocean. It is 64,000,000 square miles (165,760,000 square kilometers).

- The biggest desert in the world is the Sahara. It is 3,500,270 square miles (9,065,000 square kilometers).

BUILD YOUR VOCABULARY!

Adjectives with Negative Prefixes

They're _____ .

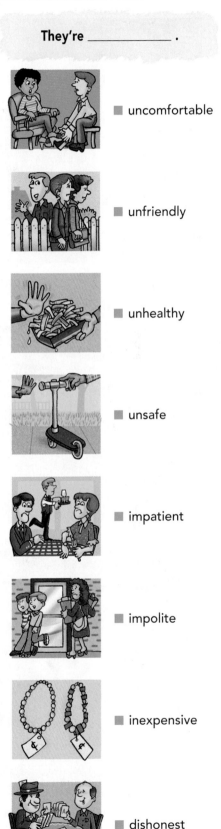

- uncomfortable
- unfriendly
- unhealthy
- unsafe
- impatient
- impolite
- inexpensive
- dishonest

Recreation and Entertainment

The most popular type of outdoor recreation in France is camping. Every night 3 million people in France sleep outside.

Movies are the most popular type of entertainment in India. Every day 15 million people in India go to the movies.

The most popular sport in the world is football. This game is called "soccer" in the United States. More than 100,000,000 people play football in over 150 countries.

What are the most popular types of recreation and entertainment in different countries you know?

Global Exchange

IvanaG: I'm going on vacation with my family tomorrow. We're going to the most popular beach in our country. We'll stay there for a week in a small hotel. It isn't the best hotel there, but it's the friendliest and the closest to the beach. We go there every year. It's a lot of fun! The water is clear, and the air is fresh. My sister and my brother and I swim all day, and we go to an amusement park in the evening. I think it has the largest roller-coaster in the world! So I'll write again when I get back and tell you all about our vacation.

P.S. Do you have a favorite vacation place? Where is it? When do you go there? What do you do?

Send a message to a keypal. Tell about a favorite vacation place in your country.

LISTENING

And Now a Word From Our Sponsors!

_b_	❶	Rings & Things	a.	furniture
____	❷	Big Value Store	b.	jewelry
____	❸	Comfort Kingdom	c.	sports equipment
____	❹	Electric City	d.	appliances
____	❺	Recreation Station	e.	home entertainment products

What Are They Saying?

The biggest!
The smallest!
The fastest!
The most exciting!

7

Imperatives
Directions

- **Getting Around Town**
- **Public Transportation**

VOCABULARY PREVIEW

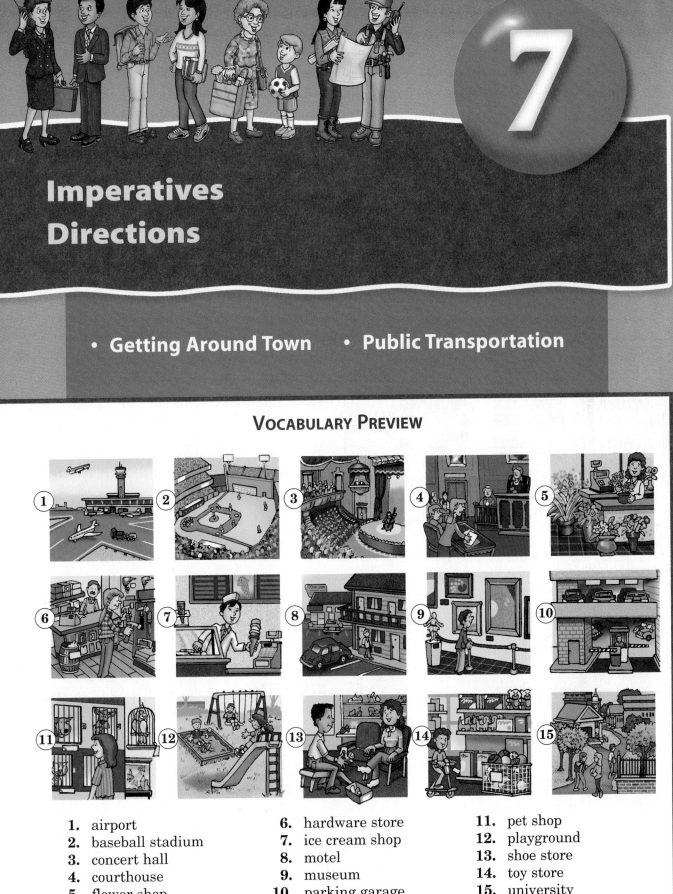

1. airport
2. baseball stadium
3. concert hall
4. courthouse
5. flower shop

6. hardware store
7. ice cream shop
8. motel
9. museum
10. parking garage

11. pet shop
12. playground
13. shoe store
14. toy store
15. university

Can You Tell Me How to Get to . . . ?

| walk up
walk down | on the right
on the left | across from
next to
between |

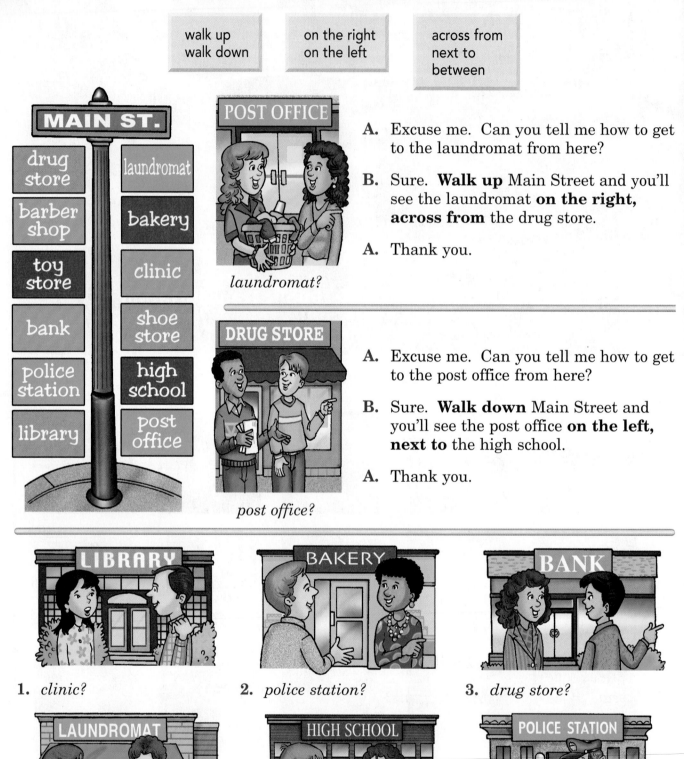

MAIN ST.

drug store	laundromat
barber shop	bakery
toy store	clinic
bank	shoe store
police station	high school
library	post office

POST OFFICE

laundromat?

A. Excuse me. Can you tell me how to get to the laundromat from here?

B. Sure. **Walk up** Main Street and you'll see the laundromat **on the right, across from** the drug store.

A. Thank you.

DRUG STORE

post office?

A. Excuse me. Can you tell me how to get to the post office from here?

B. Sure. **Walk down** Main Street and you'll see the post office **on the left, next to** the high school.

A. Thank you.

LIBRARY

1. *clinic?*

BAKERY

2. *police station?*

BANK

3. *drug store?*

LAUNDROMAT

4. *library?*

HIGH SCHOOL

5. *barber shop?*

POLICE STATION

6. *toy store?*

Could You Please Tell Me How to Get to . . . ?

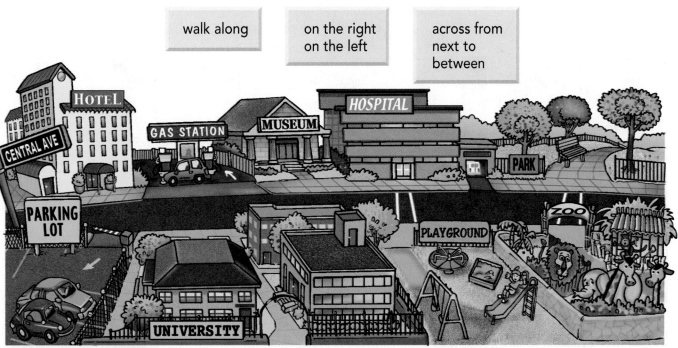

walk along	on the right on the left	across from next to between

A. Excuse me. Could you please tell me how to get to the hospital from here?

B. Sure. **Walk along** Central Avenue and you'll see the hospital **on the left, between** the museum and the park.

A. Thanks.

hospital?

1. *museum?*

2. *university?*

3. *park?*

4. *hotel?*

5. *parking lot?*

6. *zoo?*

63

Would You Please Tell Me How to Get to . . . ?

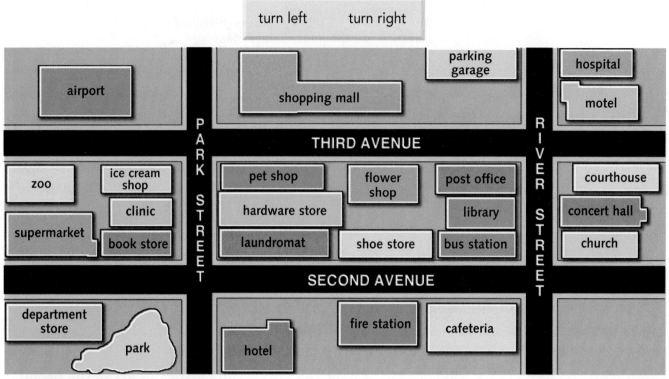

turn left	turn right

A. Excuse me. Would you please tell me how to get to the bus station from here?

B. Certainly. **Walk up** Park Street to Second Avenue and **turn right**. **Walk along** Second Avenue and you'll see the bus station **on the left, across from** the cafeteria.

A. Thanks very much.

bus station?

A. Excuse me. Would you please tell me how to get to the concert hall from here?

B. Certainly. **Drive along** Second Avenue to River Street and **turn left**. **Drive up** River Street and you'll see the concert hall **on the right, between** the courthouse and the church.

A. Thanks very much.

concert hall?

1. *hospital?*

2. *zoo?*

3. *shoe store?*

4. *laundromat?*

5. *supermarket?*

6. *post office?*

7. *clinic?*

8. *airport?*

9.

How to Say It!

Asking for Repetition

A. I'm sorry. Could you please $\left\{ \begin{array}{l} \text{repeat that?} \\ \text{say that again?} \end{array} \right.$

B. Sure. *Walk along . . .*

Practice some conversations on this page again. Ask people to repeat the directions.

Take the Main Street Bus

A. Excuse me. What's the quickest way to get to Peter's Pet Shop?

B. **Take** the Main Street bus and **get off** at First Avenue. **Walk up** First Avenue and you'll see Peter's Pet Shop **on the right**.

A. Thank you very much.

B. You're welcome.

A. Excuse me. What's the easiest way to get to Harry's Barber Shop?

B. **Take** the subway and **get off** at Fourth Avenue. **Walk down** Fourth Avenue and you'll see Harry's Barber Shop **on the left**.

A. Thank you very much.

B. You're welcome.

1. What's the fastest way to get to the baseball stadium?

2. What's the best way to get to the library?

3. What's the most direct way to get to the zoo?

4. I'm in a hurry! What's the shortest way to get to the train station?

A. Can you recommend **a good hotel**?

B. Yes. The Bellview is **a good hotel**. I think it's **one of the best hotels** in town.

A. Can you tell me how to get there?

B. Sure. Take the subway and get off at Brighton Boulevard. You'll see the Bellview at the corner of Brighton Boulevard and Twelfth Street.

A. Thank you very much.

B. You're welcome.

These people are visiting your city. Recommend real places you know and like, and give directions.

HAROLD NEVER GOT THERE!

Dear Students,

Here are directions to my house. I'll see you at the party.

Your English teacher

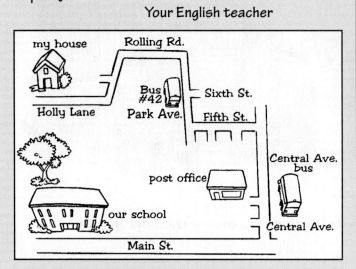

1. From our school, walk along Main St. to Central Ave. and turn left.

2. Walk up Central Ave. 2 blocks, and you'll see a bus stop at the corner, across from the post office.

3. Take the Central Ave. bus and get off at Fifth St.

4. Turn left and walk along Fifth St. 3 blocks to Park Ave. and turn right.

5. Walk up Park Ave. 1 block, and you'll see a bus stop at the corner of Park Ave. and Sixth St.

6. Take Bus #42 and get off at Rolling Rd.

7. Turn left and walk along Rolling Rd. 1 block.

8. Turn left again, and walk 2 blocks to Holly Lane and turn right.

9. Walk along Holly Lane. My house is the last one on the right.

Harold was very disappointed last night. All the other students in his English class went to a party at their teacher's house, but Harold never got there. He followed his teacher's directions, but he made one little mistake.

From their school, he walked along Main Street to Central Avenue and turned left. He walked up Central Avenue two blocks to the bus stop at the corner, across from the post office. He took the Central Avenue bus and got off at Fifth Street. He turned left and walked along Fifth Street three blocks to Park Avenue and turned right. He walked up Park Avenue one block to the bus stop at the corner of Park Avenue and Sixth Street.

He took Bus Number 42, but he got off at the wrong stop. He got off at River Road instead of Rolling Road. He turned left and walked along River Road one block. He turned left again and walked two blocks, turned right, and got completely lost.

Harold was very upset. He really wanted to go to the party last night, and he can't believe he made such a stupid mistake!

TRUE OR FALSE?

1. Harold's English teacher lives on Holly Lane.
2. The Central Avenue bus stops across from the post office.
3. The teacher made one little mistake in the directions.
4. The school is on Main Street.
5. Harold took the wrong bus.
6. Bus Number 42 goes to Rolling Road.
7. Harold got off the bus at Rolling Road.
8. Harold didn't really want to go to the party last night.

WHAT'S THE WORD?

It's very easy to get _____¹ the zoo from here. Walk up this street _____² the corner and turn right. Walk two blocks and you'll see a bus stop _____³ the corner _____⁴ Grove Street and Fourth Avenue. Take the West Side bus and get _____⁵ _____⁶ Park Road. You'll see the zoo _____⁷ the left. It's next _____⁸ the library and across _____⁹ the museum.

LISTENING

WHAT'S THE WORD?

Listen and choose the word you hear.

1. a. right   b. left
2. a. right   b. left
3. a. down   b. up
4. a. along   b. down
5. a. to   b. on
6. a. off   b. of
7. a. on   b. at

WHERE ARE THEY?

Where are these people? Listen and choose the correct place.

1. a. department store   b. laundromat
2. a. pet shop   b. cafeteria
3. a. restaurant   b. library
4. a. hospital   b. hotel
5. a. barber shop   b. supermarket
6. a. parking lot   b. parking garage

IN YOUR OWN WORDS

FOR WRITING AND DISCUSSION

You're going to invite people to your home. Draw a map and write directions to help them get there. (Give them directions from your school.)

Listen. Then say it.

Could you please tell me how to get
to the bank?

Could you please repeat that?

Would you please tell me how to get
to the library?

Say it. Then listen.

Could you please tell me how to
get to the park?

Could you please say that again?

Would you please tell me how to
get to the zoo?

SIDE *by* **SIDE**
JOURNAL

How do you get to different places in your
community? Do you walk? Do you drive?
Do you take a bus, train, or subway? Is it
easy or difficult to get to these places?
Write about it in your journal.

BUS
STOP

CHAPTER SUMMARY

GRAMMAR

IMPERATIVES

Walk up Main Street.
Turn right.
Drive along Second Avenue to River Street.

KEY VOCABULARY

PLACES AROUND TOWN

airport	cafeteria	fire station	ice cream shop	parking lot	shopping mall
bakery	church	flower shop	laundromat	pet shop	supermarket
bank	clinic	gas station	library	playground	toy store
barber shop	concert hall	hardware store	motel	police station	train station
baseball stadium	courthouse	high school	museum	post office	university
book store	department store	hospital	park	restaurant	zoo
bus station	drug store	hotel	parking garage	shoe store	

8

Adverbs
Comparative of Adverbs
Agent Nouns
If-Clauses

- Describing People's Actions
- Describing Plans and Intentions
- Consequences of Actions

VOCABULARY PREVIEW

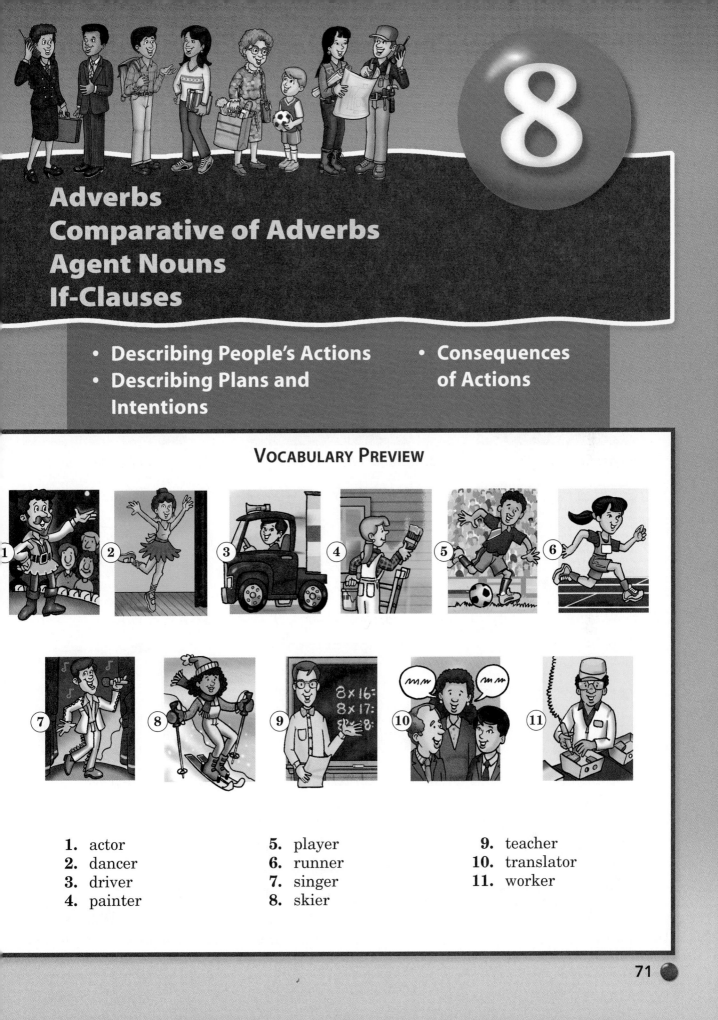

1. actor
2. dancer
3. driver
4. painter
5. player
6. runner
7. singer
8. skier
9. teacher
10. translator
11. worker

He Drives Very Carelessly

slow – slowly careless – carelessly	careful – carefully graceful – gracefully	fast – fast hard – hard	good – well

A. I think he's **a careless driver**.

B. I agree. He **drives VERY carelessly**.

1. *a careful worker*

2. *a slow chess player*

3. *a graceful dancer*

4. *good actors*

5. *a careless skier*

6. *a fast runner*

7. *a beautiful singer*

8. *bad painters*

9. *a good teacher*

10. *a hard worker*

11. *an accurate translator*

12. *dishonest card players*

You Should Work Faster

fast – faster
quickly – quicker*
loud(ly) – louder*
slowly – slower*

carefully – more carefully
gracefully – more gracefully
accurately – more accurately

well – better

A. Am I working **fast** enough?

B. Actually, you should work **faster**.

A. Am I painting **carefully** enough?

B. Actually, you should paint **more carefully**.

1. Am I typing quickly enough?

2. Am I dancing gracefully enough?

3. Am I speaking loud enough?

4. Am I driving slowly enough?

5. Am I translating accurately enough?

6. Am I playing well enough?

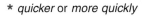

* *quicker* or *more quickly*   *louder* or *more loudly*   *slower* or *more slowly*

He Should Try to Speak Slower

loud(ly) – louder*	slowly – slower*
neatly – neater*	softly – softer*
quickly – quicker*	

| carefully – more carefully |
| politely – more politely |

| early – earlier |
| late – later |
| well – better |

A. Bob speaks VERY **quickly**.

B. You're right. He should try to speak **slower**.

1. Timothy types very slowly.

2. Carol skates very carelessly.

3. Howard speaks very softly.

4. Linda goes to bed very late.

5. Jimmy gets up very early.

6. They dress very sloppily.

7. Brenda plays her radio very loudly.

8. Richard speaks to his parents very impolitely.

9. Our next-door neighbor drives very badly.

How to Say It!

Expressing Agreement

You're right. That's right. That's true. I know. I agree. I agree with you.

Practice the conversations on this page again. Express agreement in different ways.

---

* *louder* or *more loudly*   *neater* or *more neatly*   *quicker* or *more quickly*   *slower* or *more slowly*   *softer* or *more softly*

READING

TRYING HARDER

Michael's boss talked with him today. In general, she doesn't think Michael is doing very well on the job. He has to do better. According to Michael's boss, he types too slowly. He should type faster. In addition, he files too carelessly. He should file more carefully. Furthermore, he speaks on the telephone too quickly. He should speak slower. Michael wants to do well on the job, and he knows now that he has to try a little harder.

Stella's director talked with her today. In general, he doesn't think Stella is doing very well in his play. She has to do better. According to Stella's director, she speaks too softly. She should speak louder. In addition, she walks too slowly. She should walk faster. Furthermore, she dances too awkwardly. She should dance more gracefully. Stella wants to do well in the play, and she knows now that she has to try a little harder.

Billy's teacher talked with him today. In general, she doesn't think Billy is doing very well in school. He has to do better. According to Billy's teacher, he arrives at school too late. He should arrive earlier. In addition, he dresses too sloppily. He should dress more neatly. Furthermore, he speaks too impolitely. He should speak more politely. Billy wants to do well in school, and he knows now that he has to try a little harder.

✔ READING CHECK-UP

Q & A

Michael is talking with his boss. Stella is talking with her director. Billy is talking with his teacher. Using this model, create dialogs based on the story.

A. Do I *type fast* enough?
B. No. You *type* too *slowly*.
A. Oh. I'll try to *type faster* in the future.

WHAT'S THE OPPOSITE?

1. quickly (*slowly*)
2. carefully
3. loudly
4. politely
5. badly
6. sloppily
7. awkwardly
8. earlier
9. faster

> If _____ will _____

A. What are they going to name their new baby?

B. If they have a boy, they'll name him John.
If they have a girl, they'll name her Jane.

1. A. How are you going to get to school tomorrow?

B. If it rains, I'll _____.
If it's sunny, I'll _____.

2. A. What's Roger going to do this Saturday afternoon?

B. If the weather is good, he'll _____.
If the weather is bad, he'll _____.

3. A. What's Rosa going to have for dinner tonight?

B. If she's very hungry, _____.
If she isn't very hungry, _____.

4. A. What's Ken going to do tomorrow?

B. If he feels better, _____.
If he doesn't feel better, _____.

How About You?

What are you going to do tonight if you have a lot of homework?	What are you going to wear tomorrow if it's warm and sunny?	What are you going to do this weekend if the weather is nice?
What are you going to do tonight if you DON'T have a lot of homework?	What are you going to wear tomorrow if it's cool and raining?	What are you going to do this weekend if the weather is bad?

If You Drive Too Fast, You Might Have an Accident

If _____ might _____

A. You know . . . you shouldn't drive so fast.

B. Oh?

A. Yes. If you drive too fast, you might have an accident.

B. Hmm. You're probably right.

1. *eat so quickly*
get a stomachache

2. *sing so loudly*
get a sore throat

3. *work so slowly*
lose your job

4. *go to bed so late*
be tired in the morning

5. *listen to loud music*
hurt your ears

6. *watch scary movies*
have nightmares

7. *do your homework*
so carelessly
make mistakes

8. *sit at your computer*
so long
get a backache

9.

READING

GOOD DECISIONS

Ronald wants to stay up late to watch a movie tonight, but he knows he shouldn't. If he stays up late to watch a movie, he won't get to bed until after midnight. If he doesn't get to bed until after midnight, he'll be very tired in the morning. If he's very tired in the morning, he might oversleep. If he oversleeps, he'll be late for work. If he's late for work, his boss might get angry and fire him. So, even though Ronald wants to stay up late to watch a movie tonight, he isn't going to. Good decision, Ronald!

Barbara wants to buy a new car, but she knows she shouldn't. If she buys a new car, she'll have to take a lot of money out of her bank account. If she has to take a lot of money out of her bank account, she won't have much left. If she doesn't have much left, she won't have enough money to pay the rent. If she doesn't have enough money to pay the rent, her landlord might evict her from her apartment. So, even though Barbara wants to buy a new car, she isn't going to. Good decision, Barbara!

✔ READING *CHECK-UP*

WHICH WORD IS CORRECT?

1. If Ronald (doesn't won't) go to bed early, he'll be (angry tired) in the morning.
2. If (he's he'll) late for work, his boss might (watch fire) him.
3. If Barbara (buy buys) a new car, she (won't doesn't) have much money left.
4. If she (should doesn't) pay her rent, her landlord might (account evict) her.
5. Even though Ronald and Barbara (won't want) to do these things, they (are aren't) going to.

How About You?

Complete these sentences:

If I stay up late tonight, . . .

If it rains tomorrow, . . .

If I'm not busy on Saturday, . . .

If I don't practice English, . . .

LISTENING

Listen and choose the best answer to complete the sentence.

1. a. my teacher will be happy.
   b. my teacher won't be happy.

2. a. she won't go back to school.
   b. she'll go back to school.

3. a. you'll get a sore throat.
   b. you might get a backache.

4. a. I'll be early in the future.
   b. I'll be tired in the morning.

5. a. people will hear you.
   b. people won't hear you.

6. a. your boss might fire you.
   b. your landlord might evict you.

ON YOUR OWN *Superstitions*

Many people believe that you'll have GOOD luck . . .

   if you find a four-leaf clover.
   if you find a horseshoe.
   if you give a new pair of shoes to a poor person.

Many people believe that you'll have BAD luck . . .

   if a black cat walks in front of you.
   if you walk under a ladder.
   if you open an umbrella in your home.
   if you put your shoes on a table.

Here are some other superstitions:

If your right eye itches, you'll laugh soon.
If your left eye itches, you'll cry soon.

If your right ear itches, somebody is saying good things about you.
If your left ear itches, somebody is saying bad things about you.

If a knife falls, a man will visit soon.
If a fork falls, a woman will visit soon.
If a spoon falls, a baby will visit soon.

If you break a mirror, you'll have bad luck for seven years.

Do you know any superstitions? Share them with other students in your class.

PRONUNCIATION *Contrastive Stress*

Listen. Then say it.

If it ráins, I'll go to the móvies.
If it's súnny, I'll go to the béach.

If they have a bóy, they'll name him Jóhn.
If they have a gírl, they'll name her Jáne.

If she's tíred, she'll go to bed éarly.
If she ísn't tired, she'll go to bed láte.

Say it. Then listen.

If it's hót, I'll wear a teé shirt.
If it's cóld, I'll wear a swéater.

If we work quíckly, we'll finish éarly.
If we work slówly, we'll finish láte.

If he speaks loúdly, people will héar him.
If he doésn't speak loudly, people wón't hear him.

Think about something you want to do. If you do it, what will happen? Write about it in your journal.

CHAPTER SUMMARY

GRAMMAR

ADVERBS

He works	slowly. carefully. sloppily.
	fast. hard. well.

COMPARATIVE OF ADVERBS

He should try to work	quicker. more quickly.
	more carefully. more accurately.
	faster. harder. better.

AGENT NOUNS

actor	singer
dancer	skier
driver	teacher
painter	translator
player	worker
runner	

IF-CLAUSES

If	I we you they	feel	better,	I'll we'll you'll they'll	go to work.
	he she it	feels		he'll she'll it'll	

If	I'm we're you're they're	tired,	I'll we'll you'll they'll	go to sleep early.
	he's she's it's		he'll she'll it'll	

KEY VOCABULARY

ADJECTIVES – ADVERBS

accurate – accurately
awkward – awkwardly
bad – badly
beautiful – beautifully
careful – carefully

careless – carelessly
dishonest – dishonestly
fast – fast
good – well
graceful – gracefully

hard – hard
impolite – impolitely
loud – loud(ly)
neat – neatly
polite – politely

quick – quickly
sloppy – sloppily
slow – slowly
soft – softly

You're Hired!

Ten tips for a successful job interview!

We asked personnel officers at companies in New York, Los Angeles, Toronto, Miami, Chicago, and Vancouver: What should job applicants do to have a successful job interview? Here is their advice:

1. Dress neatly. Don't dress sloppily. Comb your hair neatly.
2. Arrive promptly. Don't be late for your interview. Try to arrive early.
3. Shake hands firmly. A firm handshake shows that you are a friendly and confident person.
4. Look at the interviewer directly. Make "eye contact." Smile!
5. Listen carefully to the interviewer. Listen to the questions carefully so you can answer accurately.
6. Speak politely. Don't speak too quickly, and don't speak too loudly or softly.
7. Answer questions honestly. Tell the truth.
8. Speak confidently. Describe your skills and experience completely. If you don't have experience, you should talk about how you can learn quickly.
9. Speak enthusiastically. Show that you really want the job!
10. Send a thank-you note promptly. Thank the interviewer for his or her time and express again your interest in the job.

Some of these tips might not be correct in some cultures—for example, a firm handshake or eye contact. Are these tips correct in different cultures you know? What are other tips for job interviews in these cultures?

BUILD YOUR VOCABULARY!

Occupations

I'm a/an _____ .

- assembler
- designer
- director
- gardener
- inspector
- photographer
- programmer
- supervisor
- welder
- writer

Men and Women at Work

The jobs that men and women have are changing in many countries around the world.

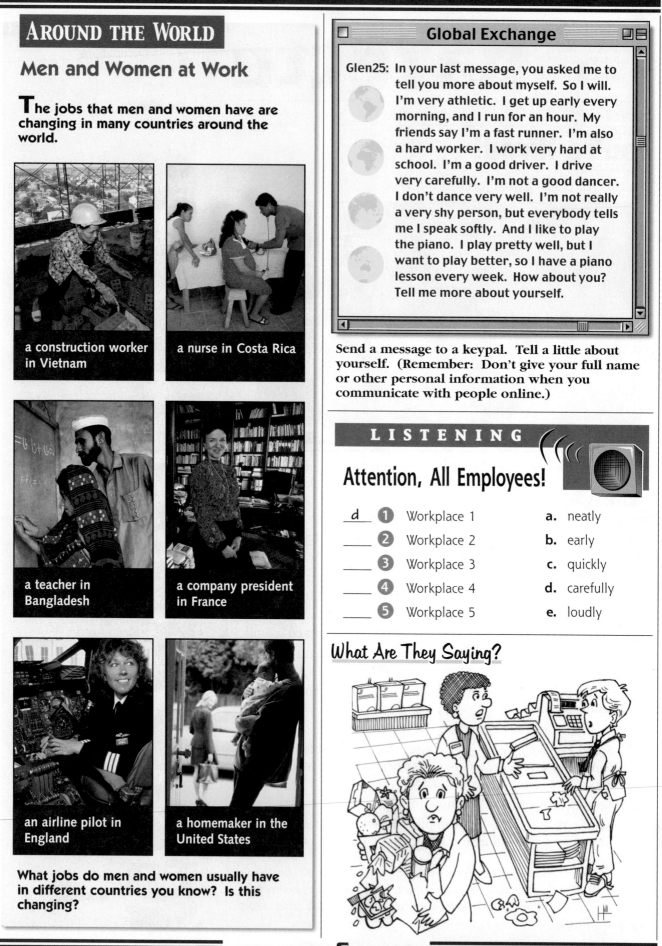

a construction worker in Vietnam

a nurse in Costa Rica

a teacher in Bangladesh

a company president in France

an airline pilot in England

a homemaker in the United States

What jobs do men and women usually have in different countries you know? Is this changing?

Global Exchange

Glen25: In your last message, you asked me to tell you more about myself. So I will. I'm very athletic. I get up early every morning, and I run for an hour. My friends say I'm a fast runner. I'm also a hard worker. I work very hard at school. I'm a good driver. I drive very carefully. I'm not a good dancer. I don't dance very well. I'm not really a very shy person, but everybody tells me I speak softly. And I like to play the piano. I play pretty well, but I want to play better, so I have a piano lesson every week. How about you? Tell me more about yourself.

Send a message to a keypal. Tell a little about yourself. (Remember: Don't give your full name or other personal information when you communicate with people online.)

LISTENING

Attention, All Employees!

_d_	① Workplace 1	**a.**	neatly
___	② Workplace 2	**b.**	early
___	③ Workplace 3	**c.**	quickly
___	④ Workplace 4	**d.**	carefully
___	⑤ Workplace 5	**e.**	loudly

What Are They Saying?

9

Past Continuous Tense
Reflexive Pronouns
While-Clauses

- **Describing Ongoing Past Activities**

VOCABULARY PREVIEW

1. bite
2. break into
3. crash into
4. drop
5. faint
6. fall
7. lose
8. spill
9. trip
10. get on
11. get off
12. get out of
13. burn myself
14. cut myself
15. hurt myself

The Blackout

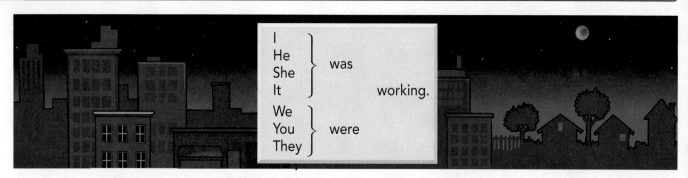

I	
He	
She	was
It	working.
We	
You	were
They	

Last night at 8:00 there was a blackout in Centerville. The lights went out all over town.

A. What was Doris doing last night when the lights went out?

B. She was taking a bath.

A. What were Mr. and Mrs. Green doing last night when the lights went out?

B. They were riding in the elevator.

1. *David*

2. *Mr. and Mrs. Park*

3. *Helen*

4. *you and your brother*

5. *you*

6. *Larry*

7. *Alice*

8. *your parents*

9. *your cousin Sam*

What were YOU doing last night at 8:00?

84

I Saw You Yesterday, but You Didn't See Me

A. I saw you yesterday, but you didn't see me.

B. Really? When?

A. At about 2:30. You were **getting out of a taxi on Main Street**.

B. That wasn't me. Yesterday at 2:30 I was **cooking dinner**.

A. Hmm. I guess I made a mistake.

1. *walking into the laundromat*
   working at my office

2. *walking out of the library*
   taking a history test

3. *getting on a bus*
   visiting my grandparents

4. *getting off a merry-go-round*
   practicing the piano

5. *jogging through the park*
   fixing my bathroom sink

6.

A ROBBERY

There was a robbery at 151 River Street yesterday afternoon. Burglars broke* into every apartment in the building while all the tenants were out.

The man in Apartment 1 wasn't home. He was washing his clothes at the laundromat. The woman in Apartment 2 wasn't home either. She was visiting a friend in the hospital. The people in Apartment 3 were gone. They were having a picnic at the beach. The man in Apartment 4 was out. He was playing tennis in the park. The college students in Apartment 5 were away. They were attending a football game. And the elderly lady in Apartment 6 was out of town. She was visiting her grandchildren in Ohio.

Yesterday certainly was an unfortunate day for the people at 151 River Street. They had no idea that while they were away, burglars broke into every apartment in the building.

* break – broke

✔ READING *CHECK-UP*

Q & A

The tenants at 151 River Street are talking to the police. Using this model, create dialogs based on the story.

A. Which apartment do you live in?
B. Apartment *1*.
A. Were you home at the time of the robbery?
B. No, *I wasn't. I was washing my clothes at the laundromat.*
A. What did the burglars take from your apartment?
B. They took *my VCR*, *my computer*, and some money I had in *a drawer in my bedroom*.
A. How much money did they take?
B. About *three hundred dollars*.

He Went to the Movies by Himself

I	myself
you	yourself
he	himself
she	herself
it	itself
we	ourselves
you	yourselves
they	themselves

A. What did **John** do yesterday?

B. He went to the movies.

A. Oh. Who did he go to the movies with?

B. Nobody. He went to the movies **by himself**.

1. *Aunt Ethel*
go to the circus

2. *your parents*
go sailing

3. *you and your wife*
have a picnic

4. *Ann*
drive to the mountains

5. *you*
go bowling

6. *your brother and sister*
play volleyball

7. *Grandma*
take a walk in the park

8. *Uncle Joe*
go fishing

9.

I Had a Bad Day Today

while

A. You look upset.

B. I had a bad day today.

A. Why? What happened?

B. I lost my wallet while I was jogging through the park.

A. I'm sorry to hear that.

A. Harry looks upset.

B. He had a bad day today.

A. Why? What happened?

B. He cut* himself while he was shaving.

A. I'm sorry to hear that.

1. *you*
hurt* myself
fixing my fence

2. *Emma*
dropped her packages
walking out of the
supermarket

3. *your parents*
got a flat tire
driving over a bridge

* cut – cut   hurt – hurt

4. Henry
tripped and fell*
walking down the stairs

5. you
burned myself
cooking on the barbecue

6. Wilma
fainted
waiting for the bus

7. you and your husband
somebody stole our car
shopping

8. you
a can of paint fell on me
walking under a ladder

9. the mail carrier
a dog bit* him
delivering the mail

How to Say It!

Reacting to Bad News

I'm sorry to hear that.

That's too bad!

That's terrible!

That's a shame!

What a shame!

What a pity!

How awful!

Practice the conversations in this lesson again. React to the bad news in different ways.

How About You?

Everybody has a bad day once in a while. Can you remember when something bad happened to you? What happened, and what were you doing when it happened?

* fall – fell   bite – bit

FRIDAY THE 13TH

Yesterday was Friday the 13th. Many people believe that Friday the 13th is a very unlucky day. I, myself, didn't think so . . . until yesterday.

Yesterday I burned myself while I was cooking breakfast.

My wife cut herself while she was opening a package.

My son poked himself in the eye while he was putting on his glasses.

Our daughter spilled milk all over herself while she was eating lunch.

Both our children fell and hurt themselves while they were roller-blading.

And we all got wet paint all over ourselves while we were sitting on a bench in the park.

I'm not usually superstitious, but yesterday was a very unlucky day. So, the next time it's Friday the 13th, do yourself a favor! Take care of yourself!

✔ READING CHECK-UP

Q & A

The man in the story is talking with a friend. Using this model, create dialogs based on the story.

    A. *My wife* had a bad day yesterday.
    B. Oh? What happened?
    A. *She cut herself* while *she was opening a package.*
    B. That's too bad!

WHICH WORD IS CORRECT?

1. He _____ himself while he was cooking.
    a. burned   b. cut
2. His daughter spilled ____.
    a. paint   b. milk
3. His son poked himself in the _____.
    a. eye   b. glasses
4. His children fell and hurt _____.
    a. ourselves   b. themselves
5. We got wet paint all over _____.
    a. ourselves   b. themselves

LISTENING

Listen to the conversations. What happened to these people? Listen and choose the correct answer.

1. a. He cut himself.
    b. He dropped his packages.
2. a. She tripped.
    b. She got a flat tire.
3. a. He burned himself.
    b. He fainted.

4. a. Somebody stole his wallet.
    b. He got paint on his pants.
5. a. They fell on the sidewalk.
    b. They hurt themselves in the basement.
6. a. He fell in the water.
    b. He spilled the water.

READING

AN ACCIDENT

I saw an accident this morning while I was standing at the corner of Park Street and Central Avenue. A man in a small red sports car was driving down Park Street very fast. While he was driving, he was talking on his cell phone. At the same time, a woman in a large green pick-up truck was driving along Central Avenue very slowly. While she was driving, she was drinking a cup of coffee and eating a donut. While the woman was driving through the intersection, the man in the sports car didn't stop at a stop sign, and he crashed into the pick-up truck. The man and the woman were very upset. While they were shouting at each other, the police came.* Fortunately, nobody was hurt badly.

* come – came

READING CHECK-UP

TRUE, FALSE, OR MAYBE?

Answer True, False, or Maybe (if the answer isn't in the story).

1. The accident happened at the corner of Park Street and Central Avenue.
2. The man was driving a small green sports car.
3. While the woman was driving, she was talking on her cell phone.
4. The man likes donuts.
5. The sports car crashed into the truck.
6. The woman was driving to work.
7. The police came after the accident.

How About You?

Tell about an accident you saw:
   Where were you?
   What happened?
   Was anybody hurt?

91

PRONUNCIATION *Did & Was*

Listen. Then say it.

What did he do?

Who did he go with?

What was he doing?

Where was she driving?

Say it. Then listen.

How did he hurt himself?

Where did he fall?

Where was she going?

Where did it happen?

Some people like to go places and do things by themselves. Others like to do things with family members and friends. How about you? Do you like to do things alone or with other people? Write about it in your journal.

CHAPTER SUMMARY

GRAMMAR

PAST CONTINUOUS TENSE

What	was	I he she it	doing?
	were	we you they	

I He She It	was	eating.
We You They	were	

REFLEXIVE PRONOUNS

I You He She It We You They	took a walk by	myself. yourself. himself. herself. itself. ourselves. yourselves. themselves.

WHILE-CLAUSES

I lost my wallet **while I was jogging through the park.**
He cut himself **while he was shaving.**

KEY VOCABULARY

VERBS

attend	crash into	faint	get on	open	stop
bite	cut *myself*	fall	get out of	poke *myself*	take a test
break into	deliver	get a flat tire	hurt *myself*	practice	take a walk
burn *myself*	drop	get off	lose	spill	trip

10

Could
Be Able to
Have Got to
Too + Adjective

- **Expressing Past and Future Ability**
- **Expressing Past and Future Obligation**
- **Giving an Excuse**

VOCABULARY PREVIEW

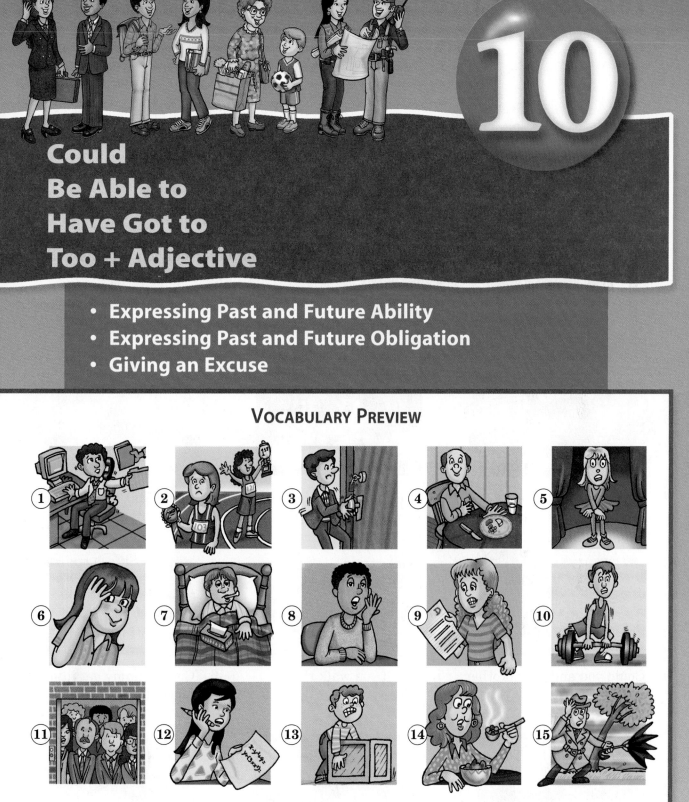

1. busy
2. disappointed
3. frustrated
4. full
5. nervous
6. shy
7. sick
8. tired
9. upset
10. weak
11. crowded
12. difficult
13. heavy
14. spicy
15. windy

They Couldn't

I
He
She
It
We
You
They

could / couldn't study.

Could he study?
Yes, he could.
No, he couldn't.

A. Could Peter play on the basketball team when he was a little boy?

B. No, he couldn't. He was too short.

1. Could Lisa go to lunch with her co-workers today?
busy

2. Could Sasha finish his homework last night?
tired

3. Could Max and Ruth finish their dinner yesterday?
full

4. Could you and your brother go to school yesterday?
sick

5. Could you walk the day after your operation?
weak

6. Could Timmy get into the movie last night?
young

7. Could Ben tell the police officer about the accident?
upset

8. Could Rita perform in school plays when she was young?
shy

9. Could Stuart and Gloria eat at their wedding?
nervous

They Weren't Able to

A. Was Jimmy able to lift his grandmother's suitcase?

B. No, he wasn't able to. It was too **heavy**.

1. Was Diane able to sit down on the subway this morning?

crowded

2. Was Charlie able to eat the food at the restaurant last night?

spicy

3. Were Nancy and Mark able to go camping last weekend?

windy

4. Were you able to solve the math problem last night?

difficult

5. Was Cathy able to find her cat last night?

dark

6. Were your parents able to swim in the ocean during their vacation?

cold

7. Was Tracy able to put her hair in a ponytail?

short

8. Was Ricky able to wear his brother's tuxedo to the prom?

small

She Had to Study for an Examination

A. Did Barbara enjoy herself at the concert last night?

B. Unfortunately, she $\left\{ \begin{array}{c} \text{wasn't able to} \\ \text{couldn't} \end{array} \right\}$ go to the concert last night. She had to **study for an examination**.

1. Did Paul enjoy himself at the tennis match last week?

visit his boss in the hospital

2. Did Amanda enjoy herself at the soccer game yesterday afternoon?

go to the eye doctor

3. Did you and your co-workers enjoy yourselves at the movies last night?

work overtime

4. Did Mr. and Mrs. Lee enjoy themselves at the symphony yesterday?

wait for the plumber

5. Did you enjoy yourself at the picnic last weekend?

work on my science project

6. Did Ralph enjoy himself at the amusement park last Sunday?

fix a flat tire

7. Did Carla enjoy herself at the school dance last Saturday night?

baby-sit for her neighbors

8.

READING

MRS. MURPHY'S STUDENTS COULDN'T DO THEIR HOMEWORK

Mrs. Murphy doesn't know what to do with her students today. They didn't do their homework last night, and now she can't teach the lesson she prepared.

Bob couldn't do his homework because he had a stomachache. Sally couldn't do her homework because she was tired and fell asleep early. John couldn't do his homework because he had to visit his grandmother in the hospital. Donna couldn't do her homework because she had to take care of her baby sister while her mother worked late at the office. And all the other students couldn't do their homework because there was a blackout in their neighborhood last night.

All the students promise Mrs. Murphy they'll be able to do their homework tonight. She certainly hopes so.

✔ READING *CHECK-UP*

Q & A

Mrs. Murphy is asking her students about their homework. Using this model, create dialogs based on the story.

A. *Bob*? Where's your homework?
B. I'm sorry, Mrs. Murphy. I couldn't do it.
A. You couldn't? Why not?
B. *I had a stomachache.*
A. Will you do your homework tonight?
B. Yes. I promise.

LISTENING

Listen and choose the correct answer.

1. a. It was too noisy.
   b. It was too crowded.

2. a. It was too windy.
   b. It was too upset.

3. a. It was too tired.
   b. It was too dark.

4. a. It was too full.
   b. It was too spicy.

5. a. They were too busy.
   b. They were too difficult.

6. a. I was too sick.
   b. I was too small.

I'm Afraid I Won't Be Able to Help You

will / won't be able to

(I have)	I've	
(We have)	We've	
(You have)	You've	
(They have)	They've	got to work.
(He has)	He's	
(She has)	She's	
(It has)	It's	

A. I'm afraid I won't be able to help you **move to your new apartment** tomorrow.

B. You won't? Why not?

A. I've got to **take my son to the doctor**.

B. Don't worry about it! I'm sure I'll be able to **move to my new apartment** by myself.

1. *paint your apartment*
   drive my parents to the airport

2. *repair your fence*
   take care of my niece and nephew

3. *study for the math test*
go to football practice

4. *set up your new computer*
fly to Denver

5. *hook up your new VCR*
take my daughter to her ballet lesson

6. *assemble Bobby's bicycle*
work late at the mall

7. *take Rover to the vet*
visit my mother in the hospital

8.

How to Say It!

Expressing Obligation

A. $\left\{\begin{array}{l}\text{I've got to}\\ \text{I have to}\\ \text{I need to}\end{array}\right\}$ take my son to the doctor.

B. Don't worry about it.

Practice the conversations in this lesson again.
Express obligation in different ways.

THE BATHROOM PIPE IS BROKEN

Mr. and Mrs. Wilson are very frustrated. A pipe broke in their bathroom yesterday while Mr. Wilson was taking a shower. They called the plumber, but she couldn't come yesterday. She was sick. She can't come today either. She's too busy. And, unfortunately, she won't be able to come tomorrow because tomorrow is Sunday, and she doesn't work on Sundays. Mr. and Mrs. Wilson are afraid they won't be able to use their shower for quite a while. That's why they're so frustrated.

THE TELEVISION IS BROKEN

Timmy Brown and his brother and sister are very frustrated. Their television broke yesterday while they were watching their favorite TV program. Their parents called the TV repairperson, but he couldn't come yesterday. He was fixing televisions on the other side of town. He can't come today either. His repair truck is broken. And, unfortunately, he won't be able to come tomorrow because he'll be out of town. Timmy Brown and his brother and sister are afraid they won't be able to watch TV for quite a while. That's why they're so frustrated.

✓ READING *CHECK-UP*

ANSWER THESE QUESTIONS

1. Could the plumber come to the Wilsons' house yesterday? Why not?
2. Can she come to their house today? Why not?
3. Will she be able to come to their house tomorrow? Why not?

4. Could the TV repairperson come to the Browns' house yesterday? Why not?
5. Can he come to their house today? Why not?
6. Will he be able to come to their house tomorrow? Why not?

CHOOSE

Mr. Wilson is calling the plumber again. Choose the correct words and then practice the conversation.

A. Hello. This is Mr. Wilson. You (have to   got to)[1] send someone to fix our bathroom pipe. I've (have to   got to)[2] take a shower!

B. I'm sorry, Mr. Wilson. You've (have to   got to)[3] understand. We (can't   aren't)[4] able to send a plumber right now. I (have to   have)[5] a big job to do on the other side of town, and my assistant (has   has to)[6] got to help me. We won't (can't   be able to)[7] come over for a few more days.

Martha is upset. She got a flat tire, and she won't be able to get to the airport on time.

Frank is frustrated. He lost his key, and he can't get into his apartment.

Emily is upset. Her computer crashed, and she lost all her work. Now she won't be able to hand in her term paper tomorrow.

Ted was really disappointed last year. He couldn't dance in the school play. His teacher said he was too clumsy.

Are you frustrated, disappointed, or upset about something? Talk about it with other students in your class.

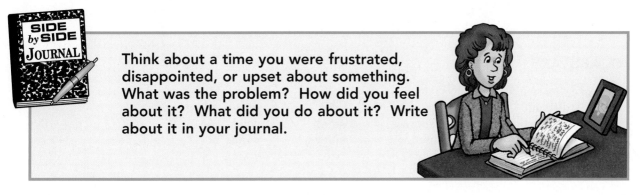

SIDE *by* **SIDE** **JOURNAL**

Think about a time you were frustrated, disappointed, or upset about something. What was the problem? How did you feel about it? What did you do about it? Write about it in your journal.

Listen. Then say it.

I have to work.

He has to go.

They've got to wait.

He's got to eat.

Say it. Then listen.

We have to study.

She has to leave.

You've got to practice.

She's got to drive.

CHAPTER SUMMARY

GRAMMAR

COULD

Could	I he she it we you they	go?

Yes,	I he she it we you they	could.

No,	I he she it we you they	couldn't.

BE ABLE TO

Was	I he she it	able to go?
Were	we you they	

No,	I he she it	wasn't	able to.
	we you they	weren't	

HAVE GOT TO

(I have) (We have) (You have) (They have)	I've We've You've They've	got to work.
(He has) (She has) (It has)	He's She's It's	

I'll He'll She'll It'll We'll You'll They'll	be able to help you.

I He She It We You They	won't be able to help you.

TOO + ADJECTIVE

He was **too short**.
She was **too busy**.

KEY VOCABULARY

ADJECTIVES

busy	difficult	heavy	sick	upset
clumsy	disappointed	nervous	small	weak
cold	frustrated	short	spicy	windy
crowded	full	shy	tired	young
dark				

Families and Time

Families have less time together

It seems that everywhere around the world, people are spending more time at work or alone and less time with their families and friends. People are busier than ever before!

In the past in many countries, the father worked and the mother stayed home, took care of the children, and did the food shopping, cooking, and cleaning. Nowadays in many families, both parents work, so they both have to do the shopping, cooking, and cleaning in their free time. Parents, therefore, don't have as much time with their children as they used to have in the past. There are also many single-parent families. In these families, the single parent has to do everything.

These days, many children come home from school to an empty apartment or house. A lot of children spend many hours each day in front of the television. Even when families are together, it is common for family members to do things by themselves. For example, they watch programs on separate TVs in different rooms, they use the Internet, they talk with friends on the telephone, and they do other individual activities.

Isn't it strange? Thanks to technology, people are able to communicate so easily with people far away, but sometimes they don't communicate as well as before with people in their own homes.

Is this happening in your country? What's your opinion about this?

FACT FILE

Countries Where People Spend the Most Time at Work

COUNTRY	HOURS OF WORK PER YEAR
Thailand	2,200
United States	1,966
Japan	1,889
France	1,656
Germany	1,560

BUILD YOUR VOCABULARY!

Home Appliances

I think the _____ is broken!

- coffee maker
- dishwasher
- dryer
- garbage disposal
- iron
- microwave
- toaster
- vacuum cleaner
- washing machine / washer

AROUND THE WORLD

Child Care

While parents around the world are working, who takes care of their young children? There are many different types of child care for pre-school children around the world.

These children are in a day-care center in their community.

These children are in a day-care center in a factory where their parents work.

This child stays home during the day with his grandmother.

What different types of child care are there in countries you know?

Global Exchange

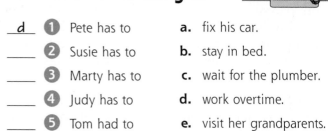

KoolKid2: Hi. It's me. I'm sorry I didn't answer your last e-mail. You won't believe what happened this week! My computer crashed, and I lost all my files—my e-mail messages, my address book, and all my schoolwork. I wasn't able to hand in the term paper for my science class yesterday because it was on my computer. I couldn't study very well for a history test because all my study notes for the exam were also on the computer. And besides all that, I tripped and fell yesterday while I was practicing for the school play. What a week! I'm glad it's over! Tell me, how was YOUR week? (I hope it was better than mine!)

Send a message to a keypal. Tell a little about your week.

LISTENING

You have five messages!

You Have Five Messages!

_d_	① Pete has to	**a.**	fix his car.
____	② Susie has to	**b.**	stay in bed.
____	③ Marty has to	**c.**	wait for the plumber.
____	④ Judy has to	**d.**	work overtime.
____	⑤ Tom had to	**e.**	visit her grandparents.

What Are They Saying?

11

Past Tense Review
Count/Non-Count Noun Review

Must
Mustn't vs. Don't Have to
Must vs. Should

- **Medical Examinations**
- **Medical Advice**
- **Health**
- **Nutrition**

VOCABULARY PREVIEW

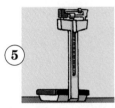

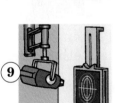

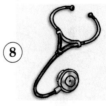

1. doctor
2. nurse
3. lab technician
4. X-ray technician

5. scale
6. weight
7. height
8. stethoscope

9. chest X-ray
10. cardiogram
11. blood pressure
12. blood test

The Checkup

You'll stand* on a scale, and the nurse will measure your height and your weight.

The nurse will take your blood pressure.

The lab technician will do some blood tests.

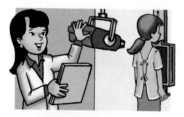

The X-ray technician will take a chest X-ray.

Then the nurse will lead* you into an examination room.

The doctor will come in, shake* your hand, and say "hello."

She'll ask you some questions about your health.

Then, she'll examine your eyes, ears, nose, and throat.

Next, she'll listen to your heart with a stethoscope.

After that, she'll take your pulse.

Then, she'll do a cardiogram.

Finally, the doctor will talk with you about your health.

* stand – stood   lead – led   shake – shook

Your Checkup

How was your medical checkup?

The doctor gave me a very complete examination.

1. I stood on a scale _____

_____

2. _____

_____

3. _____

_____

4. _____

_____

5. _____

_____

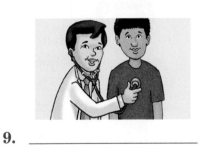

6. _____

_____

7. _____

_____

8. _____

_____

9. _____

_____

10. _____

_____

11. _____

_____

12. _____

_____

Diets

I He She It We You They	must work.

more / less	more / fewer
bread	cookies
fish	potatoes
fruit	eggs
rice	vegetables

Henry had his yearly checkup today. The doctor told him he's a little too heavy and put him on this diet:

Henry's Diet

⊖	⊕
bread	fish
cookies	vegetables
candy	fruit
potato chips	

> You must eat **less** bread, **fewer** cookies, **less** candy, and **fewer** potato chips. Also, you must eat **more** fish, **more** vegetables, and **more** fruit.

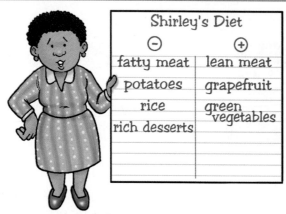

Shirley's Diet

⊖	⊕
fatty meat	lean meat
potatoes	grapefruit
rice	green vegetables
rich desserts	

Arthur's Diet

⊖	⊕
butter	margarine
eggs	yogurt
cheese	skim milk
ice cream	

1. Shirley also had her annual checkup today. The doctor told her she's a little too heavy and put her on this diet:

   She must eat _____

   _____

   _____.

2. Arthur was worried about his heart. He went to his doctor for an examination, and the doctor told him to eat fewer fatty foods.

   He must eat/drink _____

   _____

   _____.

Buster's Diet	
⊖	⊕
fatty meat	lean meat
dog biscuits	water

My Diet	
⊖	⊕

3. Buster went to the vet yesterday for his yearly checkup. The vet told him he's a little too heavy and put him on this diet:

He must eat/drink _____

_____

_____ .

4. You went to the doctor today for your annual physical examination. The doctor told you you're a little overweight and said you must go on a diet.

I must eat/drink _____

_____

_____ .

LISTENING

Listen and choose the correct word to complete the sentence.

1. a. cake
   b. cookies

2. a. bread
   b. vegetables

3. a. soda
   b. grapefruit

4. a. rice
   b. desserts

5. a. fatty meat
   b. eggs

6. a. cheese
   b. potato chips

Make a List!

What foods are good for you? What foods are bad for you? Make two lists.

Good for Me	Bad for Me

READING

CAROL'S APPLE CAKE

Carol baked an apple cake yesterday, but she couldn't follow all the instructions in her cookbook because she didn't have enough of the ingredients. She used less flour and fewer eggs than the recipe required. She also used less butter, fewer apples, fewer raisins, and less sugar than she was supposed to. As a result, Carol's apple cake didn't taste very good. As a matter of fact, it tasted terrible!

PAUL'S BEEF STEW

Paul cooked beef stew yesterday, but he couldn't follow all the instructions in his cookbook because he didn't have enough of the ingredients. He used less meat and fewer tomatoes than the recipe required. He also used fewer potatoes, less salt, less pepper, and fewer onions than he was supposed to. As a result, Paul's beef stew didn't taste very good. As a matter of fact, it tasted awful!

✔ READING *CHECK-UP*

WHAT'S THE WORD?

Steve and Judy built* their own house last year, but they couldn't follow the blueprints exactly because they didn't have enough money to buy all the construction materials they needed. They used _____1 wood and _____2 nails than the blueprints required. They also used _____3 cement, _____4 pipes, _____5 electrical wiring, and _____6 bricks than they were supposed to. As a result, their house didn't last very long. As a matter of fact, it fell down last week!

* build – built

● 110

They Must Lose Some Weight

| mustn't (must not) | don't / doesn't } have to |

A. I had my yearly checkup today.

B. What did the doctor say?

A. He said I'm a little too heavy and I must lose some weight.

B. Do you have to stop eating **ice cream**?

A. No. I don't have to stop eating **ice cream**. But I mustn't eat as much **ice cream** as I did before.

A. Grandpa had his yearly checkup today.

B. What did the doctor say?

A. She said he's a little too heavy and he must lose some weight.

B. Does he have to stop eating **cookies**?

A. No. He doesn't have to stop eating **cookies**. But he mustn't eat as many **cookies** as he did before.

1. I had my yearly checkup today.

2. Billy had his yearly checkup today.

3. Grandma had her yearly checkup today.

4. Rover had his yearly checkup today.

111

Really, Doctor?

should   must

A. I'm really worried about your heart.

B. Really, Doctor? Should I stop eating rich desserts?

A. Mr. Jones! You MUST stop eating rich desserts! If you don't, you're going to have serious problems with your heart some day.

A. I'm really worried about your _____.

B. Really, Doctor? Should I _____?

A. (Mr./Miss/Mrs./Ms.) _____! You MUST _____!
If you don't, you're going to have serious problems with your _____ some day.

1. *knees*
   stop jogging

2. *back*
   start doing exercises

3. *stomach*
   stop eating spicy foods

4. *blood pressure*
   take life a little easier

5. *hearing*
   stop listening to loud
   rock music

6.

How to Say It!

Asking for Advice

A. *I have a cold.*
{ What should I do?
  Do you have any advice?
  Do you have any suggestions? }

B. I think you should *drink some hot tea.*

Practice the conversations on this page, using these expressions for asking for advice.

INTERACTIONS

HOME REMEDIES

Different people have different remedies for medical problems that aren't very serious. For example, people do different things when they burn a finger.

Some people rub butter on their finger.

Other people put a piece of ice on their finger.

Other people put their finger under cold water.

Practice conversations with other students. Ask for advice about these medical problems, and give advice about "home remedies" you know.

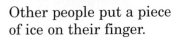
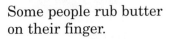

I have a cold.

I have a toothache.

I have a stomachache.

I have a bloody nose.

I have the hiccups.

Listen. Then say it.

I must eat more fruit.

He must eat fewer cookies.

You mustn't eat cake.

They mustn't eat ice cream.

Say it. Then listen.

We must eat less cheese.

She must eat more vegetables.

I mustn't eat butter.

They mustn't eat potato chips.

SIDE by **SIDE** **JOURNAL**

There are a lot of rules in daily life—things you must do and things you mustn't do. Think about the rules in YOUR life—at school, on the job, in your home, and in your community. Write about these rules in your journal.

CHAPTER SUMMARY

GRAMMAR

MUST

I He She It We You They	must work.

I He She It We You They	mustn't eat candy.

MUSTN'T VS. DON'T HAVE TO

I **don't have to** stop eating cookies.
But I **mustn't** eat as many cookies as I did before.

MUST VS. SHOULD

Should I stop eating rich desserts?
You **must** stop eating rich desserts.

COUNT/NON-COUNT NOUNS:
NON-COUNT

He must eat	more less	bread. fish. meat.

COUNT

He must eat	more fewer	cookies. potatoes. eggs.

KEY VOCABULARY

MEDICAL CHECKUP

blood pressure	height
blood test	lab technician
cardiogram	measure
checkup	neck
chest X-ray	nose
doctor	nurse
ears	scale
eyes	stethoscope
examination	throat
health	weight
heart	X-ray technician

FOODS

apples	fish	nuts	tomatoes
bread	flour	onions	vegetables
butter	french fries	pepper	water
cake	fruit	potato chips	yogurt
candy	grapefruit	potatoes	
cheese	green	raisins	fatty meat
cookies	vegetables	rice	lean meat
desserts	ice cream	salt	
dog biscuits	margarine	skim milk	
eggs	meat	sugar	

Future Continuous Tense
Time Expressions

- Describing Future Activities
- Expressing Time and Duration
- Making Plans by Telephone

VOCABULARY PREVIEW

1. bathe the dog
2. clean out the garage
3. exercise
4. iron
5. knit
6. mop the floor
7. pay bills
8. rearrange furniture
9. repaint the kitchen
10. sew
11. borrow
12. return

Will They Be Home This Evening?

(I will)	I'll
(He will)	He'll
(She will)	She'll
(It will)	It'll
(We will)	We'll
(You will)	You'll
(They will)	They'll

be working.

A. Will you be home this evening?

B. Yes, I will. I'll be reading.

1. Amanda
   ironing

2. Jack
   sewing

3. Mr. and Mrs. Kramer
   exercising

4. Omar
   paying bills

5. you
   knitting

6. Harriet
   mopping the floor

7. you and your wife
   bathing the dog

8. your parents
   rearranging furniture

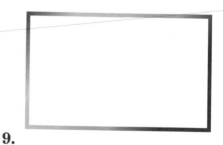

9.

Hi, Gloria. This Is Arthur.

When Can You Come Over?

Complete this conversation and practice with another student.

Hello.

Hi, _____.
This is _____.

Hi, _____. What's up?

I'm having some problems with the homework for tomorrow.

Oh. I'll be glad to help.

Thanks. I can come over at _____ o'clock. Is that okay?

I'm afraid I won't be home at _____ o'clock. I'll be _____ing. How about _____ o'clock?

No, I won't be able to come over at _____ o'clock. I'll be _____ing. How about _____ o'clock?

Fine. I'll see you then.

Will You Be Home Today at About Five O'Clock?

A. Hello, Richard. This is Julie. I want to return the tennis racket I borrowed from you last week. Will you be home today at about five o'clock?

B. Yes, I will. I'll be cooking dinner.

A. Oh. Then I won't come over at five.

B. Why not?

A. I don't want to disturb you. You'll be cooking dinner!

B. Don't worry. You won't disturb me.

A. Okay. See you at five.

A. Hello, _____. This is _____. I want to return the _____ I borrowed from you last week. Will you be home today at about _____ o'clock?

B. Yes, I will. I'll be _____ing.

A. Oh. Then I won't come over at _____.

B. Why not?

A. I don't want to disturb you. You'll be _____ing!

B. Don't worry. You won't disturb me.

A. Okay. See you at _____.

1. *videotape*
   repainting the kitchen

2. *hammer*
   cleaning out the garage

3. *football*
   ironing

4.

Calling People on the Telephone

The person you're calling is there.

A. Hello.
B. Hello. This is *David*. May I please speak to *Carol*?
A. Yes. Hold on a moment.

The person you're calling isn't there. A different person answers.

A. Hello.
B. Hello. This is *Maria*. May I please speak to *Kate*?
A. I'm sorry. *Kate* isn't here right now. Can I take a message?
B. Yes. Please tell *Kate* that *Maria* called.
A. Okay.
B. Thank you.

The person you're calling has an answering machine.

A. Hello. This is *Roger*. I'm not here right now. Please leave your name, telephone number, and a brief message after the beep, and I'll call you back. [*beep*]
B. Hi, *Roger*. This is *Eric*. . . .

Practice making telephone calls.

LISTENING

You Have Eight Messages!

Listen to the messages on Bob's machine. Match the messages.

____ 1. Aunt Betty   a. will be repainting the living room.

____ 2. Melanie   b. will be exercising at the health club.

____ 3. Alan   c. will be paying bills.

____ 4. Ms. Wong   d. will be ironing her clothes.

____ 5. Rick and Nancy   e. will be visiting Russia.

____ 6. Denise   f. will be studying for a big test.

____ 7. Dr. Garcia   g. will be working until 8 P.M.

____ 8. Mom and Dad   h. will be attending a wedding.

GROWING UP

Jessica is growing up. Very soon she'll be walking, she'll be talking, and she'll be playing with the other children in the neighborhood. Jessica can't believe how quickly time flies! She won't be a baby very much longer. Soon she'll be a little girl.

Tommy is growing up. Very soon he'll be shaving, he'll be driving, and he'll be going out on dates. Tommy can't believe how quickly time flies! He won't be a little boy very much longer. Soon he'll be a teenager.

Kathy is growing up. Very soon she'll be going to college, she'll be living away from home, and she'll be starting a career. Kathy can't believe how quickly time flies! She won't be a teenager very much longer. Soon she'll be a young adult.

Peter and Sally are getting older. Very soon they'll be getting married, they'll be having children, and they'll be buying a house. Peter and Sally can't believe how quickly time flies! They won't be young adults very much longer. Soon they'll be middle-aged.

Walter is getting older. Very soon he'll be reaching the age of sixty-five, he'll be retiring, and he'll be taking it easy for the first time in his life. Walter can't believe how quickly time flies! He won't be middle-aged very much longer. Soon he'll be a senior citizen.

✔ READING *CHECK-UP*

TRUE OR FALSE?

1. Jessica will be talking soon.
2. Kathy doesn't go to college.
3. Peter and Sally are married.
4. Walter will stop working soon.
5. Tommy is a teenager.
6. Jessica won't be going out on dates very soon.

How About You?

What do you think you'll be doing ten years from now? Tell about your future.

She'll Be Staying with Us for a Few Months

A. How long will your Aunt Gertrude be staying with us?

B. She'll be staying with us **for a few months**.

1. How long will they be staying in Vancouver?

until Friday

2. How much longer will you be working on my car?

for a few more hours

3. How late will your son be studying this evening?

until 8 o'clock

4. How much longer will you be practicing the trombone?

for a few more minutes

5. When will we be arriving in Sydney?

at 7 A.M.

6. How far will we be driving today?

until we reach Milwaukee

7. How much longer will you be chatting online with your friends?

for ten more minutes

8. How soon will Santa Claus be coming?

in a few days

HAPPY THANKSGIVING!

Thanksgiving is this week, and several of our relatives from out of town will be staying with us during the long holiday weekend. Uncle Frank will be staying for a few days. He'll be sleeping in the room over the garage. Grandma and Grandpa will be staying until next Monday. They'll be sleeping in the master bedroom. Cousin Ben will be staying until Saturday. He'll be sleeping in the guest room. Cousin Bertha will be staying for a week. She'll be sleeping on a cot in the children's bedroom. (My wife and I will be sleeping downstairs on the convertible sofa in the living room.)

Our family will be busy for the next few days. My wife and I will be preparing Thanksgiving dinner, and our children will be cleaning the house from top to bottom. We're looking forward to the holiday, but we know we'll be happy when it's over.

Happy Thanksgiving!

✔ READING *CHECK-UP*

Q & A

Uncle Frank, Grandma, Grandpa, Cousin Ben, and Cousin Bertha are calling to ask about the plans for Thanksgiving. Using this model, create dialogs based on the story.

A. Hi! This is *Uncle Frank*!
B. Hi, *Uncle Frank*! How are you?
A. Fine!
B. We're looking forward to seeing you for Thanksgiving.
A. Actually, that's why I'm calling. Are you sure there will be enough room for me?
B. Don't worry! We'll have plenty of room. You'll be sleeping *in the room over the garage*. Will that be okay?
A. That'll be fine.
B. By the way, *Uncle Frank*, how long will you be staying with us?
A. *For a few days.*
B. That's great! We're really looking forward to seeing you.

Listen. Then say it.

Yes, I will. I'll be cooking.

Yes, he will. He'll be baking.

Yes, it will. It'll be raining.

Yes, we will. We'll be reading.

Say it. Then listen.

Yes, I will. I'll be cleaning.

Yes, she will. She'll be studying.

Yes, you will. You'll be working.

Yes, they will. They'll be sleeping.

SIDE by SIDE JOURNAL

What holiday is special in your family? How do you celebrate it? Write about it in your journal.

CHAPTER SUMMARY

GRAMMAR

FUTURE CONTINUOUS TENSE

(I will)	I'll	
(He will)	He'll	
(She will)	She'll	
(It will)	It'll	be working.
(We will)	We'll	
(You will)	You'll	
(They will)	They'll	

TIME EXPRESSIONS

		a few months.
	for	a few more hours.
I'll be staying		a few more minutes.
		Friday.
	until	10 o'clock.
		we reach Milwaukee.

	at 7 A.M.
We'll be arriving	in a few days.

KEY VOCABULARY

VERBS

bathe	disturb	knit	repaint
borrow	exercise	mop	retire
clean out	grow up	pay bills	return
come over	iron	rearrange	sew

13

Some/Any
Pronoun Review
Verb Tense Review

- Offering Help
- Indicating Ownership
- Household Problems
- Friends

VOCABULARY PREVIEW

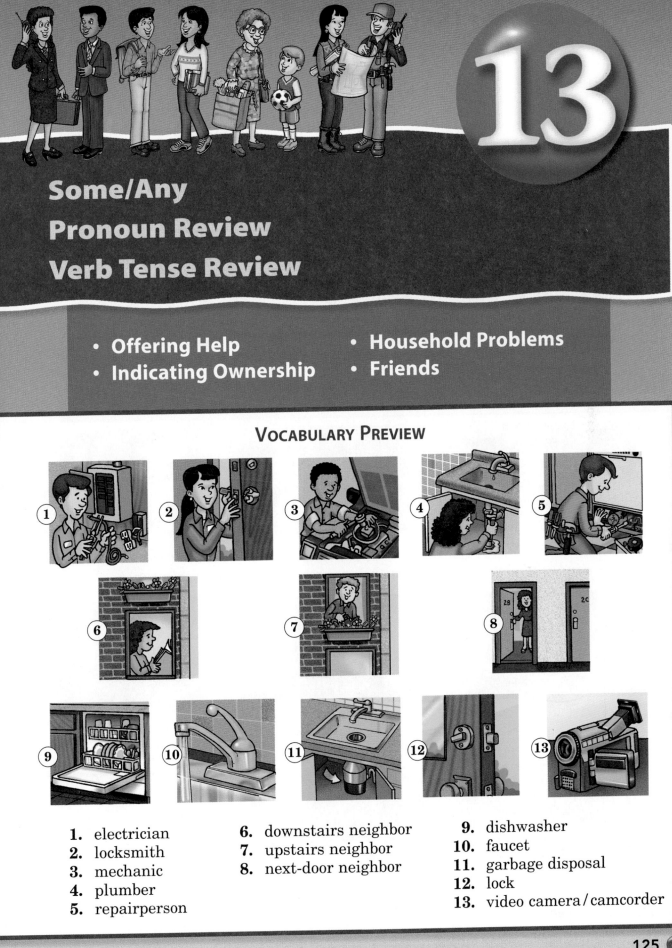

1. electrician
2. locksmith
3. mechanic
4. plumber
5. repairperson
6. downstairs neighbor
7. upstairs neighbor
8. next-door neighbor
9. dishwasher
10. faucet
11. garbage disposal
12. lock
13. video camera / camcorder

I'll Be Glad to Help

I	me	my	mine	myself
you	you	your	yours	yourself
he	him	his	his	himself
she	her	her	hers	herself
it	it	its	—	itself
we	us	our	ours	ourselves
you	you	your	yours	yourselves
they	them	their	theirs	themselves

A. What's **Johnny** doing?

B. **He's** getting dressed.

A. Does **he** need any help? I'll be glad to help **him**.

B. No, that's okay. **He** can get dressed by **himself**.

1. *your daughter feed the canary*

2. *your husband clean the garage*

3. *your children make lunch*

4. *you do my homework*

5. *your sister wash her car*

6. *Jim and Nancy rake the leaves*

7. Tom *paint the fence*

8. *you and your husband bathe the dog*

9.

 126

I Just Found This Watch

Fred

A. I just found this watch. Is it yours?

B. No, it isn't mine. But it might be **Fred's**. **He** lost **his** a few days ago.

A. Really? I'll call **him** right away.

B. When you talk to **him**, tell **him** I said "Hello."

Kate

1. *umbrella*

Alan

2. *wallet*

Grace

3. *notebook*

Mr. and Mrs. Ryan

4. *camera*

Ruth

5. *calculator*

George

6. *headphones*

Robert

7. *ring*

Jessica

8. *sunglasses*

Mr. and Mrs. Price

9. *cell phone*

Henry

10. *address book*

Janet

11. *briefcase*

12.

I Couldn't Fall Asleep Last Night

3 A.M.

A. You look tired today.

B. Yes, I know. I couldn't fall asleep last night.

A. Why not?

B. My **neighbors** were **arguing**.

A. How late did they **argue**?

B. Believe it or not, they **argued** until 3 A.M.!

A. That's terrible! Did you call and complain?

B. No, I didn't. I don't like to complain.

A. Well, I hope you sleep better tonight.

B. I'm sure I will. My **neighbors** don't **argue** very often.

1. *downstairs neighbor*
sing

2. *neighbor's* dog*
bark

3. *upstairs neighbors*
vacuum their apartment

4. *neighbors'* son*
play the drums

* neighbor – neighbor's dog
  neighbors – neighbors' son

5. neighbor across the hall
dance

6. neighbors' daughter
listen to loud music

7. next-door neighbors
rearrange their furniture

8. neighbor's cat
cry

9. neighbors' son
lift weights

10.

ON YOUR OWN *Neighbors*

Do you know your neighbors? Are they friendly? Are they helpful?
Do you sometimes have problems with your neighbors?

Talk with other students about your neighbors.

Do You Know Anybody Who Can Help Me?

something	anything
{ somebody someone }	{ anybody anyone }

A. There's something wrong with my **washing machine**.

B. I'm sorry. I can't help you. I don't know ANYTHING about **washing machines**.

A. Do you know anybody who can help me?

B. Not really. You should look in the phone book. I'm sure you'll find somebody who can fix it.

1. *refrigerator*

2. *dishwasher*

3. *kitchen faucet*

4. *garbage disposal*

5. *computer*

6. *bathtub*

7. *video camera*

8.

Can You Send a Plumber?

A. Armstrong Plumbing Company. Can I help you?

B. Yes. There's something wrong with my kitchen sink. Can you send a plumber to fix it as soon as possible?

A. Where do you live?

B. 156 Grove Street in Centerville.

A. I can send a plumber tomorrow morning. Is that okay?

B. Not really. I'm afraid I won't be home tomorrow morning. I'll be taking my son to the dentist.

A. How about tomorrow afternoon?

B. Tomorrow afternoon? What time?

A. Between one and four.

B. That's fine. Somebody will be here then.

A. What's the name?

B. Helen Bradley.

A. And what's the address again?

B. 156 Grove Street in Centerville.

A. And the phone number?

B. 237-9180.

A. Okay. We'll have someone there tomorrow afternoon.

B. Thank you.

A. _____. Can I help you?

B. Yes. There's something wrong with my _____.
Can you send a _____ to fix it as soon as possible?

A. Where do you live?

B. _____ in _____.

A. I can send a _____ tomorrow morning. Is that okay?

B. Not really. I'm afraid I won't be home tomorrow morning.
I'll be _____ing.

A. How about tomorrow afternoon?

B. Tomorrow afternoon? What time?

A. Between _____ and _____.

B. That's fine. Somebody will be here then.

A. What's the name?

B. _____.

A. And what's the address again?

B. _____ in _____.

A. And the phone number?

B. _____.

A. Okay. We'll have someone there tomorrow afternoon.

B. Thank you.

1. _Ajax Home Electronics Service_
repairperson

2. _Ace Electrical Repair_
electrician

3. _Patty's Plumbing and Heating_
plumber

4. _Larry's Lock Repair_
locksmith

TROUBLE WITH CARS

It might seem hard to believe, but my friends and I are all having trouble with our cars. There's something wrong with all of them!

Charlie is having trouble with his. The brakes don't work. He tried to fix them by himself, but he wasn't able to, since he doesn't know anything about cars. Finally, he took the car to his mechanic. The mechanic charged him a lot of money, and the brakes STILL don't work! Charlie is really annoyed. He's having a lot of trouble with his car, and he can't find anybody who can help him.

Betty is having trouble with hers. It doesn't start in the morning. She tried to fix it by herself, but she wasn't able to, since she doesn't know anything about cars. Finally, she took the car to her mechanic. The mechanic charged her a lot of money, and the car STILL doesn't start in the morning! Betty is really annoyed. She's having a lot of trouble with her car, and she can't find anybody who can help her.

Mark and Nancy are having trouble with theirs. The steering wheel doesn't turn. They tried to fix it by themselves, but they weren't able to, since they don't know anything about cars. Finally, they took the car to their mechanic. The mechanic charged them a lot of money, and the steering wheel STILL doesn't turn! Mark and Nancy are really annoyed. They're having a lot of trouble with their car, and they can't find anybody who can help them.

I'm having trouble with mine, too. The windows don't go up and down. I tried to fix them by myself, but I wasn't able to, since I don't know anything about cars. Finally, I took the car to my mechanic. The mechanic charged me a lot of money, and the windows STILL don't go up and down! I'm really annoyed. I'm having a lot of trouble with my car, and I can't find anybody who can help me.

133

✓ READING CHECK-UP

WHAT'S THE WORD?

1. Charlie tried to fix _____ car by _____.

2. Mark and Nancy's mechanic charged _____ a lot and still didn't fix _____ car.

3. Betty can't find anybody to help _____ fix _____ car.

4. I'm having trouble with _____ car, too. _____ starts in the morning, but the windows are broken.

5. The windows don't go up and down. I tried to fix _____ by _____, but I couldn't.

6. My friends and I can't fix _____ cars by _____, and we're all very angry at _____ mechanics.

LISTENING

WHAT'S THE WORD?

Listen and choose the word you hear.

1. a. him   b. her
2. a. him   b. them
3. a. them   b. him
4. a. yours   b. hers
5. a. yourself   b. yourselves
6. a. our   b. her

WHAT ARE THEY TALKING ABOUT?

Listen and choose what the people are talking about.

1. a. stove   b. sink
2. a. dishwasher   b. garbage disposal
3. a. TV   b. camcorder
4. a. headphones   b. cell phone
5. a. windows   b. car

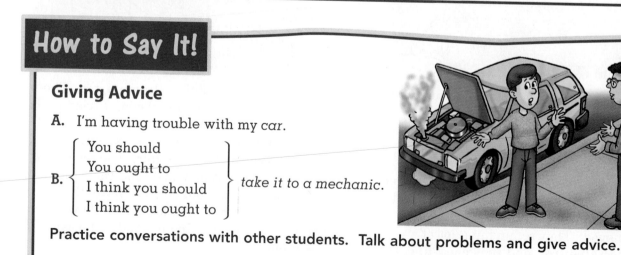

How About You?

Are you "handy"? Do you like to fix things? Tell about something you fixed. What was the problem? How did you fix it? Also, tell about something you COULDN'T fix. What was the problem? What did you do?

How to Say It!

Giving Advice

A. I'm having trouble with my car.

B. {
You should
You ought to
I think you should
I think you ought to
} take it to a mechanic.

Practice conversations with other students. Talk about problems and give advice.

IN YOUR OWN WORDS

THAT'S WHAT FRIENDS ARE FOR!

Frank has some very nice friends. He sees his friends often. When he needs help, they're always happy to help him. For example, last week Frank moved to a new apartment. He couldn't move everything by himself, and he didn't really have enough money to hire a moving company. His friends came over and helped him move everything. He was very grateful. His friends said, "We're happy to help you, Frank. That's what friends are for!"

Emma has some very special friends. She sees her friends often. When she needs help, they're always happy to help her. For example, last month the faucet broke in Emma's kitchen and flooded her apartment. There was water in every room. She couldn't fix everything herself, and her superintendent didn't help her at all. Her friends came over and helped her fix the faucet and clean up every room in the apartment. She was very grateful. Her friends said, "We're happy to help you, Emma. That's what friends are for!"

It's nice to have friends you can rely on when you need help. Tell about a time when your friends helped you. Tell about a time when you helped a friend.

PRONUNCIATION Deleted *h*

Listen. Then say it.

Tell him I said "Hello."

I'll be glad to help him.

He can get dressed by himself.

The mechanic charged him a lot of money.

Say it. Then listen.

Tell her I said "Hello."

I'll be glad to help her.

She can make lunch by herself.

The mechanic charged her a lot of money.

SIDE by SIDE JOURNAL

Think about a very good friend. Write about this person in your journal.

CHAPTER SUMMARY

GRAMMAR

PRONOUN REVIEW

Subject Pronouns	Object Pronouns	Possessive Adjectives	Possessive Pronouns	Reflexive Pronouns
I	me	my	mine	myself
you	you	your	yours	yourself
he	him	his	his	himself
she	her	her	hers	herself
it	it	its	—	itself
we	us	our	ours	ourselves
you	you	your	yours	yourselves
they	them	their	theirs	themselves

SOME/ANY

There's **something** wrong with my washing machine.
I'm sure you'll find **somebody/someone** who can fix it.

I don't know **anything** about washing machines.
Do you know **anybody/anyone** who can help me?

POSSESSIVE OF SINGULAR & PLURAL NOUNS

neighbor – neighbor's dog
neighbors – neighbors' son

KEY VOCABULARY

OCCUPATIONS

dentist
electrician
locksmith
mechanic
plumber
repairperson

OBJECTS

address book
brakes
dishwasher
faucet
garbage disposal
headphones
lock
phone book
steering wheel
video camera / camcorder

Communities

Some communities are friendly, and some aren't

There are many different kinds of communities around the world. Communities can be urban (in a city), suburban (near a city), or rural (in the countryside, far from a city).

Urban communities usually have many neighborhoods, where people often live close together in apartment buildings or small houses. Streets in these neighborhoods often have lots of people and many stores and businesses. People in urban neighborhoods often walk or take public transportation to get to places.

In suburban communities, people typically live in separate houses. Stores and businesses are not usually nearby, and people often have to drive to get there. Some suburban communities have public transportation, and others don't.

In rural communities, people often live far apart from each other, not in neighborhoods. There isn't usually any public transportation, and people have to drive everywhere.

Whether in urban, suburban, or rural areas, some communities are friendly, and others aren't. For example, in some communities, people know their neighbors, they help each other, and their children play together all the time. In other communities, people keep to themselves and sometimes don't even know their neighbors' names.

In the old days, most people around the world lived in small towns and villages, where they knew their neighbors. These days, more people live in large urban communities. Experts predict that in the future most people will live in "megacities" of more than ten million people. Will there be friendly neighborhoods in these communities of the future? Time will tell.

Describe your community. Is it urban, suburban, or rural? Is it friendly? In your opinion, what will your community be like in the future?

FACT FILE

The Ten Largest Cities in the World: 1950 and 2010 (Population in Millions)

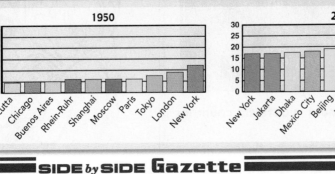

1950 — Calcutta, Chicago, Buenos Aires, Rhein-Ruhr, Shanghai, Moscow, Paris, Tokyo, London, New York

2010 — New York, Jakarta, Dhaka, Mexico City, Beijing, Lagos, Shanghai, Mumbai,* Sao Paolo, Tokyo

*formerly Bombay

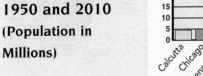

Where Friends Get Together

These friends are meeting in the plaza in the center of Guanajuato, Mexico.

These friends are meeting at a coffee shop in Los Angeles.

These friends are talking in a park in Shanghai.

Where do friends meet in different countries you know?

Global Exchange

JuanR: I'm really looking forward to next weekend. Our family will be celebrating my grandparents' fiftieth wedding anniversary! Everybody in my family will be there—my parents, my brothers and sisters, and all my aunts, uncles, and cousins. We're going to have a big dinner at our home. Then, all the grandchildren will present a play that tells the story of my grandparents' lives together. (I'm going to be my grandfather when he was 20 years old!) We're going to have music and dancing, and we're going to give them a special anniversary present—a book of photographs of our whole family through the years. I'll tell you all about the party in my next message.

Send a message to a keypal. Tell about a family celebration you're looking forward to.

LISTENING

Who Are They Calling?

_c_ **①** Amy Francis   **a.** mechanic

____ **②** Paul Mendoza   **b.** locksmith

____ **③** Jim Carney   **c.** plumber

____ **④** Jennifer Park   **d.** electrician

____ **⑤** Ed Green   **e.** carpenter

What Are They Saying?

APPENDIX

Listening Scripts

Chapter 1 – Page 9

Listen and choose the correct answer.

1. What are you going to do tomorrow?
2. What do you do in the summer?
3. When did you clean your apartment?
4. What did you give your parents for their anniversary?
5. Where did you and your friends go yesterday?
6. How often do they send messages to each other?
7. What did he give her?
8. When are you going to make pancakes?

Chapter 2 – Page 16

Listen and choose what the people are talking about.

1. A. How much do you want?
   B. Just a little, please.
2. A. Do you want some more?
   B. Okay. But just a few.
3. A. These are delicious!
   B. I'm glad you like them.
4. A. I ate too many.
   B. How many did you eat?
5. A. They're bad for my health.
   B. Really?
6. A. It's very good.
   B. Thank you.
7. A. Would you care for some more?
   B. Yes, but not too much.
8. A. There isn't any.
   B. There isn't?!

Chapter 3 – Page 22

Listen and choose what the people are talking about.

1. A. How much does a gallon cost?
   B. Two seventy-nine.
2. A. They're very expensive this week.
   B. You're right.
3. A. How many loaves do we need?
   B. Three.
4. A. Sorry. There aren't any more.
   B. There aren't?!
5. A. I need two pounds.
   B. Two pounds? Okay.
6. A. How much does the large box cost?
   B. Five thirty-nine.
7. A. How many cans do we need?
   B. Three.
8. A. I bought too much.
   B. Really?

Side by Side Gazette – Page 28

Listen and match the products and the prices.

1. Attention, food shoppers! Thank you for shopping at Save-Rite Supermarket! Crispy Cereal is on sale this week. A box of Crispy Cereal is only three dollars and forty-nine cents. Three forty-nine is a very good price for Crispy Cereal. So buy some today!
2. Attention, shoppers! Right now in the bakery section whole wheat bread is on sale. Buy a loaf of whole wheat bread for only two seventy-five. That's right! Just two seventy-five! The bread is hot and fresh. So come to the bakery section and get a loaf now!
3. Thank you for shopping at Sunny Supermarket! We have a special low price on orange juice today. A quart of orange juice is only a dollar seventy-nine. Orange juice is in Aisle 5, next to the milk.
4. Hello, food shoppers! It's 95 degrees today. It's a good day for Sorelli's ice cream! Sorelli's ice cream comes in vanilla, chocolate, and other delicious flavors. And today, a pint of Sorelli's ice cream is only three twenty-five!
5. Welcome to Bartley's Supermarket! We have a special today on bananas. You can buy bananas for only forty cents a pound. Bananas are good for you! So walk over to our fruit section and buy a bunch of bananas today!

Chapter 4 – Page 37

WHAT'S THE LINE?

Mrs. Harris (from the story on page 36) is calling Tommy and Julie's school. Listen and choose the correct lines.

1. Good morning. Park Elementary School.
2. Yes, Mrs. Harris. What can I do for you?
3. Oh? What's the matter?
4. That's too bad. Are you going to take them to the doctor?
5. Well, I hope Tommy and Julie feel better soon.

WHAT'S THE WORD?

Listen and choose the word you hear.

1. I might go to school tomorrow.
2. I want to come to work today.
3. Don't walk there!
4. We'll be ready in half an hour.
5. They'll go to school tomorrow.
6. Don't stand there! You might get hit!
7. I call the doctor when I'm sick.
8. Watch your step! There are wet spots on the floor.
9. I'm sick and tired of sailing.

Chapter 5 – Page 44

Listen and choose what the people are talking about.

1. A. I like it. It's fast.
   B. It is. It's much faster than my old one.

2. A. Is it comfortable?
   B. Yes. It's more comfortable than my old one.

3. A. I think it should be shorter.
   B. But it's very short now!

4. A. They aren't very polite.
   B. You're right. They should be more polite.

5. A. Is it safe?
   B. Yes. It's much safer than my old one.

6. A. Which one should I buy?
   B. Buy this one. It's more powerful than that one.

Chapter 6 – Page 53

Listen to the sentence. Is the person saying something good or something bad about someone else?

1. She's the nicest person I know.
2. He's the laziest student in our class.
3. He's the most boring person I know.
4. She's the most generous person in our family.
5. They're the most honest people I know.
6. He's the rudest person in our apartment building.
7. He's the most dependable person in our office.
8. She's the kindest neighbor on our street.
9. She's the most stubborn person I know.

Side by Side Gazette – Page 60

Listen and match the products.

ANNOUNCER: Are you looking for a special gift for a special person in your life? A birthday gift? An anniversary present? Come to Rings & Things—the best store in town for rings, necklaces, earrings, bracelets, and other fine things. Rings & Things—on Main Street downtown, or at the East Side Mall.

FRIEND 1: That was an excellent dinner!
FRIEND 2: Thank you. I'm glad you liked it.
FRIEND 1: Can I help you wash the dishes?
FRIEND 2: Thanks. But they're already in the dishwasher.
FRIEND 1: Is your dishwasher on?
FRIEND 2: Yes, it is.
FRIEND 1: I can't believe it! Your dishwasher is MUCH quieter than mine.
FRIEND 2: It's new. We got it at the Big Value Store. They sell the quietest dishwashers in town.
ANNOUNCER: That's right. The Big Value Store sells the quietest dishwashers in town. We also have the largest refrigerators, the most powerful washing machines, and the best ovens. And we also have the best prices! So come to the Big Value Store, on Airport Road, open seven days a week.

PERSON WHO CAN'T FALL ASLEEP: Oh, I can't believe it! It's three o'clock in the morning, and I can't fall asleep.

This bed is so uncomfortable! I need a new bed. I need a new bed NOW!
ANNOUNCER: Do you have this problem? Is your bed uncomfortable? Come to Comfort Kingdom for the most comfortable beds you can buy. We also have the most beautiful sofas and the most attractive tables and chairs in the city. And our salespeople are the friendliest and the most helpful in town. So visit Comfort Kingdom today because life is short, and you should be comfortable!

ANNOUNCER: I'm standing here today in front of Electric City so we can talk to a typical customer. Here's a typical customer now. He's leaving the store with a large box. Let's ask him a question. Excuse me, sir. May I ask you a question?
CUSTOMER: Certainly.
ANNOUNCER: What did you buy today?
CUSTOMER: A VCR.
ANNOUNCER: And why did you buy it at Electric City?
CUSTOMER: Because Electric City has the cheapest and the most dependable products in town.
ANNOUNCER: Is this your first time at Electric City?
CUSTOMER: Oh, no! Last year I bought a radio here, and the year before I bought a TV.
ANNOUNCER: And are you happy with those products?
CUSTOMER: Absolutely! The radio is much better than my old one, and the picture on my TV is much bigger and brighter.
ANNOUNCER: So are you a happy customer?
CUSTOMER: Definitely! There's no place like Electric City. It's the best store in town.
ANNOUNCER: Well, there you have it! Another happy Electric City customer. Visit an Electric City store near YOU today!

ANNOUNCER: This is it! It's the biggest sale of the year, and it's this weekend at Recreation Station! That's right. Everything is on sale—sneakers, tennis rackets, footballs, basketballs—everything in the store! It's all on sale at Recreation Station. We're the largest! We're the most convenient! We're the best! And this weekend we're the cheapest! It's the biggest sale of the year, and it's this weekend—only at Recreation Station!

Chapter 7 – Page 69

WHAT'S THE WORD?

Listen and choose the word you hear.

1. The clinic is on the right, next to the post office.
2. The library is on the left, across from the park.
3. Walk up Town Road to Main Street.
4. Drive along Fourth Avenue to Station Street.
5. Take the subway to Pond Road.
6. The bus stop is at the corner of Central Avenue and Fifth.
7. Take this bus and get off at Bond Street.

WHERE ARE THEY?

Where are these people? Listen and choose the correct place.

1. A. Do you want to buy this shirt?
   B. Yes, please.
2. A. Please give me an order of chicken.
   B. An order of chicken? Certainly.
3. A. Shh! Please be quiet! People are reading.
   B. Sorry.
4. A. Can I visit my wife?
   B. Yes. She and the baby are in Room 407.
5. A. How much does one head cost?
   B. A dollar fifty-nine.
6. A. Hmm. Where's our car?
   B. I think it's on the third floor.

Chapter 8 – Page 79

Listen and choose the best answer to complete the sentence.

1. If I do my homework carelessly, . . .
2. If Sally doesn't feel better soon, . . .
3. If you sit at your computer for a long time, . . .
4. If I stay up late tonight, . . .
5. If you don't speak loudly, . . .
6. If you don't work hard, . . .

Side by Side Gazette – Page 82

Listen to these announcements at different workplaces. Match the workplace and the word you hear.

Attention, all employees! This is Ms. Barnum, the factory supervisor. There were three accidents in our factory last week. Nobody was hurt badly, but I worry about these accidents. Please try to work more carefully. Thank you for your attention.

Attention, all employees! There is a small fire in the building. Please walk quickly to the nearest exit! Don't run! I repeat: There is a small fire in the building. Please walk quickly to the nearest exit!

May I have your attention, please? The president of our company will visit our office tomorrow. Please dress neatly for her visit. Thank you.

Cut! Okay, everybody! That was good, but you're still singing too softly. Please try to sing more loudly. Okay? Let's try that again.

Attention, please! As you know, the weather is very bad this afternoon, and according to the weather forecast, the storm is going to get worse. Therefore, we are going to close the office early today. All employees can leave at three thirty. Get home safely! See you tomorrow.

Chapter 9 – Page 91

Listen to the conversations. What happened to these people? Listen and choose the correct answer.

1. A. How did you do that?
   B. I did it while I was shaving.
2. A. When did it happen?
   B. While I was getting off a bus.
3. A. Why do you think it happened?
   B. It was a very hot day.
4. A. The park isn't as safe as it used to be.
   B. You're right.
5. A. What were they doing?
   B. They were playing outside.
6. A. How did it happen?
   B. He dropped the glass.

Chapter 10 – Page 97

Listen and choose the correct answer.

1. I couldn't sit down on the bus.
2. Tony wasn't able to paint his house.
3. Jennifer couldn't find her purse last night.
4. They didn't enjoy the food at the restaurant.
5. Why weren't the plumbers able to fix it?
6. Why couldn't you go to work yesterday?

Side by Side Gazette – Page 104

Listen to the messages on Jim's machine. Match the people and their messages.

You have five messages.

Message One, Friday, 2:15 P.M.: Hi, Jim. This is Pete. I just got your message. I'm sorry I won't be able to help you move to your new apartment tomorrow, but I've got to work overtime. 'Bye. [*beep*]

Message Two, Friday, 3:10 P.M.: Hi, Jim. It's Susie. Sorry I won't be able to help you move tomorrow. I've got to visit my grandparents out of town. Good luck! Talk to you soon. [*beep*]

Message Three, Friday, 3:55 P.M.: Jim? Hi. It's Marty! How are you? I'm not so good. I'm having problems with my car. I have to take it to a mechanic, so I'm afraid I won't be able to help you move. Sorry. Give me a call sometime. Okay? Take care. [*beep*]

Message Four, Friday, 5:48 P.M.: Hello, Jim? It's Judy. You know, I really want to help you move, but I've got to stay home all day tomorrow and wait for the plumber. My kitchen sink is broken, and there's water everywhere! Hope your move goes okay. Sorry I can't help. Let's talk soon. [*beep*]

Message Five, Sunday, 9:29 P.M.: Jim? It's Tom. Gee, I'm really sorry I wasn't able to help you move yesterday. I wasn't feeling well, and I had to stay in bed all day. I'm feeling much better now. Call me. Maybe we can get together soon. [*beep*]

Chapter 11 – Page 109

Listen and choose the correct word to complete the sentence.

1. A. I had my yearly checkup today.
   B. What did the doctor say?
   A. She said I must eat fewer . . .

2. A. I had my annual checkup today.
   B. What did the doctor say?
   A. He said I must eat less . . .

3. A. How was your medical checkup?
   B. Okay. The doctor said I must drink less . . .

4. A. Did the doctor put you on a diet?
   B. Yes. She said I must eat fewer . . .

5. A. I went to my doctor for an examination today.
   B. Oh. What did the doctor say?
   A. He said I must eat less . . .

6. A. My doctor put me on a diet today.
   B. Really?
   A. Yes. I must eat fewer . . .

Chapter 12 – Page 120

Listen to the messages on Bob's machine. Match the messages.

You have eight messages.

Message Number One: "Hello, Robert. This is Aunt Betty. I'm calling to say hello. Call me back. I'll be home all evening. I'll be ironing my clothes. Talk to you soon. 'Bye." [*beep*]

Message Number Two: "Hi, Bob. This is Melanie. I'm making plans for the weekend. Do you want to do something? Call me when you have a chance. I'll be home all day. I'll be studying for a big test. Talk to you later." [*beep*]

Message Number Three: "Bob? This is Alan. What's up? I'm calling to tell you I won't be able to play tennis with you this Saturday. I'll be attending my cousin's wedding in Dallas. See you soon." [*beep*]

Message Number Four: "Hello, Mr. Kendall. This is Ms. Wong from the State Street Bank. I'm calling about your application for a loan. We need some more information. Please call me at 472-9138. You can call this evening. I'll be working until 8 P.M. Thank you." [*beep*]

Message Number Five: "Hi, Bob. This is Rick. Nancy and I want to invite you over to dinner at our new apartment. Call us back. We'll be home all weekend. We'll be repainting the living room. Bye." [*beep*]

Message Number Six: "Hello, Bob. This is Denise. I got your message last week. Sorry I missed you. Call me back. I'll be home this evening. I'll be paying bills. Take care." [*beep*]

Message Number Seven: "Hello. This is a message for Robert Kendall. I'm calling from Dr. Garcia's office. Dr. Garcia won't be able to see you next month. He'll be visiting hospitals in Russia. Please call so we can change your appointment. Thank you, and have a nice day." [*beep*]

Message Number Eight: "Hello, Bobby? This is Mom. Bobby, are you there? Pick up the phone. I guess you aren't there. Dad and I are thinking of you. How are you? Call us, okay? But don't call this afternoon. We'll be exercising at the health club. Well, talk to you soon, Bobby. 'Bye." [*beep*]

Chapter 13 – Page 134

WHAT'S THE WORD?

Listen and choose the word you hear.

1. Do you know him well?
2. I'll be glad to help them.
3. Did you see him today?
4. Yours will be ready at five o'clock.
5. Careful! You might hurt yourselves!
6. We're having trouble with her car.

WHAT ARE THEY TALKING ABOUT?

Listen and choose what the people are talking about.

1. I'm going to have to call the plumber.
2. It's broken. We won't be able to wash the dishes.
3. I'm upset. I can't watch my favorite program.
4. It doesn't work. I can't call anybody!
5. My mechanic fixed the brakes.

Side by Side Gazette – Page 138

Listen to the messages and conversations. Match the caller with the repairperson.

1. A. Hello. This is Dan, the Drain Man. I'm not here to take your call. Please leave your name, number, and the time you called. Also, please describe the problem. I'll get back to you as soon as possible. Have a great day!
   B. Hello. This is Amy Francis. My number is 355-3729. It's three o'clock Friday afternoon. My kitchen faucet is broken. I can't turn off the water! Please call back as soon as possible. Thank you.

2. A. Hello. This is Helen's Home Repair. If you break it, we can fix it! Nobody is here right now. Leave a message after the beep, and we'll call you back. Thank you.
   B. Hi. This is Paul Mendoza. My front steps are broken, and I need somebody who can fix them. My phone number is 266-0381. Please call back soon. I'm having a party this weekend, and nobody will be able to get into my house! Thank you.

3. A. Hi. This is Kevin's Key Service. Leave a message and I'll call you back. Thanks.

   B. Good morning. My name is Jim Carney. I'm really embarrassed. I just lost my keys while I was jogging, and I can't get into my apartment. I'm calling from my neighbor's apartment across the hall. I live at 44 Wilson Road, Apartment 3B. My neighbor's number is 276-9184. Please call back soon. Thank you.

4. A. Gary's Garage. May I help you?

   B. Yes. I think there's something wrong with my steering wheel.

   A. What's the problem?

   B. It's difficult to turn right, and it's VERY difficult to turn left!

   A. Hmm. That's not good. What's your name?

   B. Jennifer Park.

   A. Phone number?

   B. 836-7275.

   A. Can you be here tomorrow morning at eight?

   B. Yes. That's fine. Thank you.

5. A. Hello. Rita's Repair Company.

   B. Hi. Is this Rita?

   A. No. This is the answering service. May I help you?

   B. Yes. My doorbell is broken. It won't stop ringing!

   A. I can hear that. Your name, please?

   B. Ed Green.

   A. Address?

   B. 2219 High Street.

   A. And your phone number?

   B. 923-4187.

   A. Will someone be home all day?

   B. Yes. I'll be here.

   A. Okay. Rita will be there before 5 P.M.

   B. Thank you.

Thematic Glossary

pre-school 104
pretty 40
proud 52
quick 66
quiet 25
ready 30
real 46
reasonable 57
reliable 46
rich 112
ridiculous 45
right 43
romantic 25
rude 49
sad 32
safe 40
satisfied 44
scary 77
separate 103
serious 112
short 44
shy 82
sick 9
single 103
sloppy 49
slow 72
small 27
smart 39
soft 39
special 24
spicy 39
strange 103
stubborn 49
stupid 68
suburban 137
successful 81
superstitious 90
sure 35
sympathetic 44
talented 39
talkative 39
tall 47
tasty 25
terrible 17
tired 22
ugly 52
uncomfortable 59
understanding 44
unfortunate 86
unfriendly 59
unhealthy 59
unlucky 90
unsafe 59
upset 16
urban 137
used 42
useful 42

weak 93
wet 90
wide 47
wonderful 15
worried 108
worse 56
worst 56
wrong 68
yearly 108
young 94

Describing with Adverbs

accurately 73
always 8
awkwardly 75
badly 74
beautifully 80
better 73
carefully 72
carelessly 72
completely 68
confidently 81
directly 81
dishonestly 80
early 74
easily 103
enthusiastically 81
exactly 110
fast 72
firmly 81
gracefully 72
hard 72
honestly 81
impolitely 74
late 74
loud 73
loudly 73
neatly 74
never 8
often 8
on time 101
politely 74
promptly 81
quickly 73
sloppily 74
slowly 72
softly 74
sometimes 129
soon 24
usually 28
well 72

Entertainment and the Arts

ballet lesson 99
dancing 138
entertainment 60
jazz 5
movie 43

music 44
piano lesson 43
radio talk show 46
rock music 5
symphony 96
TV program 58

Events and Occurrences

accident 77
anniversary 7
birthday 6
blackout 84
celebration 59
concert 96
costume party 59
date 25
holiday weekend 123
party 24
picnic 35
play 75
prom 95
robbery 86
Thanksgiving 123
vacation 33
wedding anniversary 25
wedding 94

Family Members

aunt 50
brother 30
children 7
cousin 50
daughter 6
family 5
family members 103
father 4
grandchildren 7
grandfather 51
Grandma 123
grandmother 2
Grandpa 123
grandparent 85
husband 6
mother 32
nephew 51
niece 98
parent 7
relative 123
single-parent family 103
sister 50
son 44
uncle 50
wife 6

Food Containers and Quantities

bag 19
bottle 19
bowl 23

box 19
bunch 19
can 19
cup 23
dish 23
dozen 19
gallon 19
glass 23
half a pound 19
half pound 19
head 19
jar 19
loaf 19
order 23
piece 23
pint 19
pound 19
quart 19
slice 27

Foods

appetizer 25
apple cake 110
apple pie 13
apple 11
bagel 27
baked chicken 25
baking soda 24
banana 11
beef stew 110
bread 11
broiled fish 25
butter 12
cake 11
candy 6
carrot 11
cereal 19
cheese 8
chicken 11
chicken soup 23
chili 27
chocolate bar 27
chocolate cake 15
chocolate ice cream 23
cocoa beans 27
coffee 12
cookie 12
donut 27
egg 11
fish 11
flavor 28
flour 12
food 17
french fries 13
fruit 27
fruitcake 24
grapefruit 108
grapes 11

hamburger 13
honey 24
hot chocolate 23
hot dog 27
ice cream 12
jam 19
ketchup 11
lemon 11
lemonade 13
lettuce 11
margarine 108
mayonnaise 11
meat 11
meatball 13
meatloaf 41
milk 12
muffin 27
mushroom 24
mustard 11
nut 24
omelet 13
onion 11
orange 8
orange juice 12
pancake 4
pear 11
pepper 11
pizza 13
potato 11
potato chips 108
raisin 24
rice 12
roll 28
salad 13
salt 11
sandwich 13
scrambled eggs 23
skim milk 108
snack 28
soda 12
soup 19
soy sauce 11
spaghetti 4
stew 24
strawberry 23
sugar 12
Swiss cheese 21
taco 27
tea 12
tomato 11
tomato juice 25
vanilla ice cream 23
vegetable 17
vegetable soup 25
vegetable stew 24
water 24
white bread 19

whole wheat bread 19
yogurt 12

Geography

country 58
desert 59
island 27
mountain 59
ocean 59
river 59
world 27

Getting Around Town

avenue 63
block 68
boulevard 67
directions 68
intersection 91
lane 68
left 62
location 56
public transportation 137
right 62
road 68
sidewalk 91
stop 68
stop sign 91
street 46

Home

apartment 33
apartment building 41
appliance 56
basement 91
bathroom 85
bathroom pipe 100
bathroom sink 85
bathtub 130
bed 22
bedroom 33
cabinet 12
cable TV 137
condominium 8
convertible sofa 123
cot 123
counter 12
dishwasher 40
downstairs 51
faucet 125
floor 115
freezer 12
furniture 45
garage 115
garbage disposal 103
garden 32
guest room 123
home 22
home appliance 103

150

fork 79
four-leaf clover 79
grass 32
groceries 16
hammer 119
headphones 127
home entertainment products 56
horseshoe 79
ice 59
ingredient 110
instructions 110
iron 103
items 27
key 101
knife 79
ladder 79
leaves 126
letter 5
lights 84
list 12
location 56
magazine 58
mail 89
map 69
merry-go-round 85
mirror 79
mixing bowl 24
nails 110
newspaper 58
novel 45
package 88
paint 89
painting 7
people 31
perfume 6
phone book 130
photograph 138
piano 3
plant 7
polka dots 7
ponytail 95
present 6
product 56
radio 54
recipe 24
roller coaster 35
saucepan 24
shopping list 20
spoon 79
story 32
suitcase 95
table 25
telephone 75
thank-you note 81
thing 60
tip 81
toaster 103

ton 27
toothpaste 53
tree 32
trombone 122
TV 2
VCR 86
video 4
video camera 55
videotape 119
water 60
wig 40
window 133
wire 34
wood 110
world 27

Occupations

actor 58
actress 58
airline pilot 82
assembler 81
assistant 100
carpenter 138
chef 24
chimneysweep 137
company president 82
construction worker 82
dancer 53
dentist 131
designer 81
director 75
doctor 15
driver 71
electrician 125
exterminator 137
eye doctor 96
gardener 81
homemaker 82
house painter 137
inspector 81
installer 137
lab technician 105
landlord 50
locksmith 125
mail carrier 89
mayor 46
mechanic 125
newspaper carrier 137
nurse 82
painter 71
personnel officer 81
photographer 81
pilot 82
player 71
plumber 96
police officer 94
president 82

professor 43
programmer 81
repairperson 125
runner 71
senator 51
singer 58
skier 71
superintendent 135
supervisor 81
teacher 24
translator 71
TV repairperson 100
TV star 58
vet (veterinarian) 99
waiter 25
waitress 25
welder 81
worker 71
writer 81
X-ray technician 105

Parts of the Body

arm 36
back 112
ears 77
eyes 34
feet 35
finger 113
hair 44
hand 43
head 34
heart 106
knees 112
leg 35
nose 106
stomach 112
throat 77

People

adult 121
baby 76
boss 45
boy 32
burglar 86
co-worker 94
everybody 82
girl 52
guest 30
lady 86
man 79
neighbor 51
nobody 87
people 31
person 50
police 86
relative 123
salespeople 56

Cardinal Numbers

1	one	20	twenty
2	two	21	twenty-one
3	three	22	twenty-two
4	four	.	.
5	five	.	.
6	six	29	twenty-nine
7	seven	30	thirty
8	eight	40	forty
9	nine	50	fifty
10	ten	60	sixty
11	eleven	70	seventy
12	twelve	80	eighty
13	thirteen	90	ninety
14	fourteen		
15	fifteen	100	one hundred
16	sixteen	200	two hundred
17	seventeen	300	three hundred
18	eighteen	.	.
19	nineteen	.	.
		900	nine hundred
		1,000	one thousand
		2,000	two thousand
		3,000	three thousand
		.	.
		10,000	ten thousand
		100,000	one hundred thousand
		1,000,000	one million

Ordinal Numbers

1st	first	20th	twentieth
2nd	second	21st	twenty-first
3rd	third	22nd	twenty-second
4th	fourth	.	.
5th	fifth	.	.
6th	sixth	29th	twenty-ninth
7th	seventh	30th	thirtieth
8th	eighth	40th	fortieth
9th	ninth	50th	fiftieth
10th	tenth	60th	sixtieth
11th	eleventh	70th	seventieth
12th	twelfth	80th	eightieth
13th	thirteenth	90th	ninetieth
14th	fourteenth		
15th	fifteenth	100th	one hundredth
16th	sixteenth	1,000th	one thousandth
17th	seventeenth	1,000,000th	one millionth
18th	eighteenth		
19th	nineteenth		

How to Read a Date

June 9, 1941 = "June ninth, nineteen forty-one"

November 16, 2010 = "November sixteenth, two thousand ten" *or*

"November sixteenth, two thousand and ten"

Irregular Verbs: Past Tense

be	was	lead	led
become	became	leave	left
begin	began	lend	lent
bite	bit	lose	lost
break	broke	make	made
build	built	meet	met
buy	bought	put	put
catch	caught	read	read
come	came	ride	rode
cost	cost	run	ran
cut	cut	say	said
do	did	see	saw
drink	drank	sell	sold
drive	drove	send	sent
eat	ate	shake	shook
fall	fell	sing	sang
feed	fed	sit	sat
feel	felt	sleep	slept
find	found	speak	spoke
fly	flew	spend	spent
forget	forgot	stand	stood
get	got	steal	stole
give	gave	swim	swam
go	went	take	took
grow	grew	teach	taught
have	had	tell	told
hear	heard	think	thought
hurt	hurt	understand	understood
keep	kept	wear	wore
know	knew	write	wrote

Index